THE ATLANTA CAMPAIGN

A Civil War Driving Tour
of
Atlanta-Area Battlefields

by

J. BRITT McCARLEY

with

**A Reader's Guide to the
Atlanta Campaign**

by

Stephen Davis & Richard M. McMurry

Originally published as a special issue of the *Atlanta Historical Journal* (now *Atlanta History: A Journal of Georgia and the South*), a publication of the Atlanta Historical Society.

Cherokee Publishing Company
Atlanta, Georgia
1989

Library of Congress Cataloging-in-Publication Data

McCarley, J. Britt.
  The Atlanta Campaign : Atlanta is ours and fairly won" : a driving tour of the Atlanta area's principle
Civil War battlefields with a reader's guide to the Atlanta Campaign / by J. Britt McCarley.
    p.   c.m.
  A revision of a special issue of the Atlanta historical journal,
vol. XXVIII, no. 3, Fall 1984.
  Bibliography: p.
  Includes index.
  ISBN 0-87797-160-9 (alk. paper)   : $8.95 (est.)
    1. Atlanta Campaign, 1864. 2. Historic sites--Georgia--Atlanta Region--Guide-books. 3. Atlanta
Region (Ga.)--Description and travel--Guide-books. 4. Georgia--History--Civil War, 1861-1865--
Battlefields--Guide-books. 5. United States--History--Civil War, 1861-1865--Battlefields--Guide-books.
6. Automobiles--Road guides--Georgia--Atlanta Region.   I. Title.
E476.7.M33 1988   88-18941
973.7'37--dc19   CIP

Copyright © 1984 by the Atlanta Historical Society, Inc.

This book is printed on acid-free paper which conforms to the American National Standard Z39.48-
1984 *Permanence of Paper for Printed Library Materials.* Paper that conforms to this standard's
requirements for pH, alkaline reserve and freedom from groundwood is anticipated to last several
hundred years without significant deterioration under normal library use and storage conditions. ∞

Manufactured in the United States of America

First Edition

ISBN: 0-87797-160-9

98 97 96 95 94   10 9 8 7 6 5 4 3 2

Index by Alexa Selph

Cover design by Paulette Lambert

Edited by Bradley R. Rice and Jane Powers Weldon

Coordinated by Elizabeth Thurman Speir, Director of Publications

Published by arrangement with the Atlanta Historical Society, Inc.

Cover paintings by Wilbur G. Kurtz

 Cherokee Publishing Company is an operating division of the
Larlin Corporation, P.O. Box 1730, Marietta, Georgia 30061

Table of Contents

1984 Preface

Any Atlantan or visitor to the city who is even casually interested in history knows that the Union forces of General William T. Sherman captured Atlanta in 1864 in one of the key campaigns of the Civil War. Only ardent buffs and scholars, however, know exactly where the major encounters took place and even fewer have systematically visited the sites. Only the most dedicated historian, amateur or professional, could read through all of the published material concerning the Atlanta campaign. This special issue of the *Atlanta Historical Journal* is designed to make both the sites and the literature accessible to a broad audience of metropolitan residents and tourists.

Numerous people in and out of the Atlanta Historical Society helped on this project. The key person who kept it all tied together, as she does for so many things, was Publications Director Jane Powers Weldon. Society Director John H. Ott paved the way for final map and manuscript preparation by providing tour author Britt McCarley with a summer internship. He also read the tour text and made some helpful suggestions. Other Society stalwarts who read the manuscript and shared their ideas were Historian Franklin Garrett, Museum Director Robert Kothe, and Chairman Beverly DuBose. Photographer William Fulmer Hull cheerfully and skillfully took the present-day photographs that accompany the tour. Jean Marchman and Ann Watson helpfully typed part of the manuscript. Education Director Madeline Reamy Patchen also expedited the internship through the Education and Publications Departments of the Atlanta Historical Society.

An early version of the tour was prepared by Britt McCarley while he was an intern with the Atlanta Urban Design Commission under the supervision of the late Jenny Thurston. Professor Timothy J. Crimmins of Georgia State University arranged that internship and then worked to make sure that the project could be completed here.

Britt McCarley, who received his master's from Georgia State, is now a doctoral student in military history at Temple University in Philadelphia. His major professor, Russell F. Weigley, has given much helpful direction. In addition, Professor Roderick E. McGrew, also of Temple, and Daniel A. Brown, historian at Stone's River National Military Park, were kind enough to read the paper and offer their suggestions.

The "Reader's Guide" portion of this issue was prepared by two scholars who are well known to the readers of the *Atlanta Historical*

Journal for their previous articles about the Civil War in and about Atlanta. Stephen Davis is a member of the journal's editorial board, and Richard McMurry is the author of the acclaimed *John Bell Hood and the War for Southern Independence.* They have provided a quick and useful overview of the literature that will serve as a starting place for further reading.

Bradley R. Rice

Editor's Note: Britt McCarley received his Ph.D. in American military history in 1988 from Temple University.

"Atlanta Is Ours and Fairly Won": A Driving Tour of the Atlanta Area's Principal Civil War Battlefields

By J. Britt McCarley

Introduction

This automobile tour of the four major Civil War battlefield sites around Atlanta has several purposes. Each of the short tours, designed as a series of four, will take a few hours at most to complete. The tours are not intended to be definitive accounts of the battles they treat; rather, the goal has been to provide a general understanding of each of the battles and their places in the struggle for Atlanta in the summer of 1864. All along the tour routes, there are many historical markers erected by the now-dissolved Georgia Historical Commission. These plaques provide an in-depth description of the battles and can be used by anyone wishing to gain deeper knowledge of Atlanta's Civil War battlefields.

For convenience and safety, the narrative should be read by a companion who is not driving. All the material needed to take the tours is provided here. Be sure to read through each section, beginning with the brief description of the battle and then proceeding to read the driving tour itself. Once this is accomplished, go over the map ahead of time, so you will know what to look for in an area before you get there. Use the maps and rosters of troops to keep up with units and their locations. Additionally, in order that the reader might more easily differentiate

* The contents of the Atlanta Campaign historical plaques are largely correct, but they are occasionally misplaced. This minor drawback, however, does not detract from their usefulness.

Accompanying this tour is a bibliographic essay by Stephen Davis and Richard M. McMurry. The essay discusses and lists primary and secondary sources about the Atlanta Campaign. Particularly useful sources in preparing these tours were *The Official Records of the War of the Rebellion;* the military memoirs of Generals Sherman, Johnston, and Hood; *Georgia Historical Markers* (the complete text of the state's historical tablets); Thomas Lawrence Connelly's *Autumn of Glory: The Army of Tennessee, 1862-1865;* and Stanley F. Horn's *The Army of Tennessee.*

Southern and Northern commanders and units, the names of Confederate officers and units are italicized. The positioning of troops has been noted with reference to present-day roads, parks, and structures. The right and left of a unit are determined as an officer at that time would have viewed the situation from his lines. On each map there is an arrow pointing northward.

The Atlanta Campaign: May 5 to July 20, 1864

Of the four years comprising the American Civil War, 1864 proved to be the most decisive militarily. The campaigns and battles of that year brought the greatest amount of destruction to the waning Confederacy and its military forces. In late March, Gen. Ulysses S. Grant,* who had been elevated to the command of all the Northern armies on March 9 by Pres. Abraham Lincoln, met with Gen. William T. Sherman to formulate the grand strategy for the approaching campaigning season. Their plans would bring to completion the tenets of the so-called "Anaconda Plan," the imprecise strategic scheme for encircling and subdividing the South that Gen. Winfield Scott, commander of the United States Army from the beginning of the war until his retirement due to bad health on October 31, 1861, had designed.

As it evolved through the war, the Anaconda policy came to include three basic objectives: first, blockade the southern coastline with the Union navy; second, divide the South along the Mississippi River and through the interior from the Tennessee River to the Atlantic; third, capture the Confederate capital at Richmond. As of early 1864, the Union had come a long way toward subduing its foe. The whole length of the Mississippi was securely in Union hands, and nearly all the South's ports were sealed off from outside contact. Also, after having successfully blunted repeated Confederate forays northward from Tennessee and Virginia, Federal forces stood poised in Chattanooga and in northern Virginia for the final assault upon the remaining citadels of the Confederacy.

The result of the March 1864 deliberations of Grant and Sherman was the decision for a coordinated series of spring offensives by all the Union field armies with the common goal of destroying their Confederate counterparts and seizing and rendering useless important southern cities, railroad networks, and centers of manufacturing. To accomplish these objectives, two main thrusts were planned, one aimed at Richmond and the Southern forces defending it and the other at the Confederate Army of Tennessee in Georgia. In the vicinity of Richmond,

---

* All general officers, regardless of their specific grade, will be referred to in the text simply as "General." The full grade of each general is given in the tables of forces engaged that accompany each tour.

the Union advance was directed toward capturing that city by way of a march up the south bank of the James River by Gen. Benjamin F. Butler's Army of the James.* Another Federal thrust would be carried out by the Army of the Potomac, under the day-to-day command of Gen. George G. Meade but directed strategically by General Grant. The mission of this army was to pin down and destroy Confederate Gen. *Robert E. Lee's* Army of Northern Virginia. In the Deep South, Federal movements would be commanded by General Sherman and directed against Gen. *Joseph E. Johnston's* Army of Tennessee encamped in the vicinity of Dalton, Georgia.

Sherman's instructions for the part he would play came from Grant on April 4:

> You I propose to move against *Johnston's* army, [Grant directed] to break it up, and to get into the interior of the enemy's country as far as you can, inflicting all the damage you can against their war resources.

Therefore, Sherman was charged with two responsibilities. Besides the stated objective of destroying *Johnston's* army, the order implied that Atlanta, commonly referred to as the workshop and warehouse of the Confederacy with its industrial facilities and railroad complex, should

The "car shed" of the Western and Atlanta Railroad. This view symbolizes Atlanta's role as the transportation hub of the western Confederacy. (Library of Congress [LC] photograph.)

---

* Union armies were usually named after rivers, i.e., the Army of *the* Cumberland or the Army of *the* Tennessee. They varied in size from about 15,000 to 60,000. Confederate armies, on the other hand, were most often named after states, i.e., the Army of Tennessee and the Army of Mississippi. The size of Southern armies varied as much as that of their Northern counterparts. Armies were further divided into units ranging downward in size from corps to divisions to brigades and then to regiments for infantry and cavalry and batteries for artillery.

be captured and destroyed. If all these movements were successful, Grant and Sherman reasoned, the Confederacy would be sliced into several pieces which would be unable to function as a whole, thus bringing an end to the war.

The Atlanta Campaign may have been the key element in the war's final year. The capture of Atlanta exerted a major influence on Lincoln's reelection. His victory in the war-weary year of 1864 constituted a rejection of compromise with the South and ensured that the conflict would continue to a definite conclusion despite the already-staggering losses on both sides.

Earlier fighting in the late summer and early fall of 1863 had led to Federal control of Chattanooga and paved the way for a successful campaign in Georgia by Sherman. Beginning in the last two weeks of August of that year, Union forces under Gen. William S. Rosecrans left their positions in central Tennessee and headed for Chattanooga, intending to pry Gen. *Braxton Bragg's* Confederate army out of what was one of the most important transportation and communication hubs in the South. Crossing the Tennessee River in early September, Rosecrans's bluecoats fanned out over the countryside of northwest Georgia. Their aim was to cut the communication and supply lines from the heart of Georgia that provided sustenance for *Bragg's* army. *Bragg* was reported to be retreating from Chattanooga to protect the very umbilical cord threatened by Rosecrans.

Indeed, *Bragg* was not in Chattanooga, but neither was he withdrawing southward. His army was positioned about ten miles south, around Lee and Gordon's Mill on Chickamauga Creek. With relative ease, *Bragg* could have defeated the various detachments of Rosecrans's forces, but the dilatory response by the Confederates resulted in a lost opportunity. Once alerted to the danger of a concentrated foe in his front, Rosecrans assembled his forces, and the two sides faced each other for the impending clash of arms. The resulting Battle of Chickamauga, fought on September 19 and 20, 1863, ended in a decisive rout of the Union forces from the field as a result of a fortuitous attack by Confederate reinforcements from Virginia, under the command of Gen. *James B. Longstreet*, into a portion of the Federal line temporarily lacking defenders. The heroic stand of Union troops under the direct command of Gen. George H. Thomas, one of the North's most able leaders, saved Rosecrans's army from complete disaster. Thomas shielded the retreat of the rest of the· army from the field and then withdrew his troops into Chattanooga, where *Bragg* clamped the city's Union defenders in a siege. *Bragg*, however, missed yet another opportunity when he failed to assault the disorganized and fleeing Federals streaming into Chattanooga. (The United States National Park Service, a unit of the Department of the Interior, preserves these battlefields in the Chickamauga-Chattanooga National Military Park. The headquarters of the park can be reached by driving north on Interstate 75 from Atlanta and taking the exit marked Chickamauga Battlefield. The entire Atlanta Campaign and Sherman's March to the Sea in late 1864 are portrayed in the Georgia Campaign Diorama at Stone Mountain Park, which is located fifteen miles east of Atlanta.)

The Union's response to this desperate situation was to organize reinforcements in Mississippi, Western Tennessee, and Virginia and rush them as fast as possible to Chattanooga. In mid-October, Rosecrans was relieved of his command by Grant, who in turn was installed as commander of the newly created Military Division of the Mississippi. When Grant arrived on the scene, the Federal forces in Chattanooga, including the horses and mules, were on starvation rations. Grant's chief engineer, Gen. William F. "Baldy" Smith, organized a special operation to open a temporary supply line. Carried out in late October, the plan opened the so-called "Cracker Line," a supply link to provisions for animals and men stockpiled in northern Alabama. Now well supplied, Grant and his subordinates, who by this time included Sherman, planned and executed in late November a series of attacks against *Bragg's* army, and the siege was broken. More troops and supplies from the North flowed into Chattanooga, and preparations began for Sherman's Atlanta Campaign that would commence the following spring.

To carry out his mission, Sherman, who had been elevated to command the Military Division of the Mississippi upon Grant's promotion to Lieutenant-General, had at his disposal three armies totaling nearly 110,000 men. From largest to smallest, they were General Thomas's Army of the Cumberland, the Army of the Tennessee under Gen. James B. McPherson, and the Army of the Ohio with Gen. John M. Schofield in command. Instead of trying to force the enemy back by direct assault, Sherman's strategy during the Atlanta Campaign called for the use of flanking marches to compel the Confederates to abandon their entrenched positions.

Though he did not know precisely what Sherman's intentions were, *Johnston*, who replaced *Bragg* during the winter of 1863-64 after the battles that broke the Confederate siege of Chattanooga, adopted a defensive plan well suited to the size of his army* and the terrain over which he expected to march and fight. Since north Georgia is predominantly mountainous, *Johnston* chose to rely on heavily fortified field entrenchments that were laid out and dug in advance under the supervision of Confederate engineers. By such a strategy, *Johnston* expected to use his trenches as a base from which to strike out and defeat por-

---

* *Johnston's* army initially numbered only about 52,000 men but later swelled to around 70,000 as reinforcements arrived from elsewhere in the Confederacy. At the beginning of the campaign, the *Army of Tennessee* was originally composed of two and later three infantry corps and attached troops under Gens. *Leonidas Polk, William J. Hardee,* and *John B. Hood.*

MAP 1. (Maps 1-3 are reproduced with permission of the Kennesaw Mountain Historical Association from Richard M. McMurry's history of the Atlanta Campaign of 1864, *The Road Past Kennesaw* (National Park Service, 1972).

tions of the Union army that might become detached from the main body and therefore be vulnerable to counterattack.

With their separate strategies in mind, *Johnston* and Sherman anxiously awaited the coming of spring and the onset of good campaigning weather. His armies equipped and ready, Sherman marched out of Chattanooga on May 5, 1864, to open the campaign. The first encounter between the Northern and Southern armies was indicative of the course of events through most of the first eleven weeks of the campaign. Thomas's and Schofield's armies, in the initial movements against the Southerners, entrenched themselves in front of *Johnston's* forces on Rocky Face Ridge, just north of the Confederate winter camp at Dalton. Seeing that it would be too costly to take the Southern position on the ridge by storm, Sherman dispatched McPherson's army on a flanking march to the south by way of a passage through the mountains known as Snake Creek Gap. Some of *Johnston's* units at Resaca, south

of Dalton, brushed with McPherson's troops, and word was quickly sent
to *Johnston* that an attempt was being made to sever the Western and
Atlantic (W&A) Railroad, the Confederate supply line extending north
from Atlanta. During the early morning hours of May 13, the Confederates at Rocky Face left their trenches and marched south to Resaca,
thus preserving their lines of retreat and supply. Except for an arduous
week of fighting in the thickly forested areas around Dallas, New Hope,
and Pickett's Mill (which is currently being developed as a battlefield
park by the state of Georgia), the campaign continued in a similar fashion of orderly strategic retreat. During the third week of June, the
Army of Tennessee withdrew to the Kennesaw Mountain line north of
Marietta, where two weeks were spent in numerous skirmishes and
fights. Up to this point in the campaign, the losses suffered by both
sides were nearly equal at approximately 11,000 each.

On June 27, Sherman departed from his usual flanking tactics and
decided to launch a direct assault on portions of the Confederate lines
at Kennesaw. The heaviest Union attacks came at Pigeon Hill, a small
rise adjoining the southern peak of Kennesaw Mountain and a few
miles south at a hillock known then as the "Dead Angle" because of a

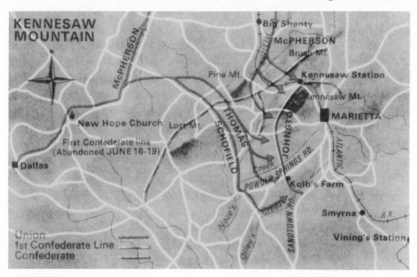

MAP 2.

sharp and exposed curve in the Confederate line. The purpose of these
frontal assaults was to pierce *Johnston's* line at several supposedly
weak points and thereby to destroy the Army of Tennessee. The attacks
were a miserable failure, costing the Federals 3,000 casualties and the
Confederates only 600. Having learned a valuable lesson, Sherman re-
verted to his dependable flanking maneuvers again on July 2. (The
Kennesaw Mountain National Battlefield Park, a unit of the National
Park Service, can be reached by taking Interstate 75 about twenty miles

north from downtown Atlanta. The exit is marked. Near the mountain is the small town of Kennesaw. Within its city limits is the Big Shanty Museum, which commemorates the Great Locomotive Chase, also known as Andrews's Raid, of April 12, 1862. Housed within the museum is the General, the locomotive used in the raid.)

After being flanked out of the Kennesaw line, the Confederates fought several skirmishes with Federal forces from fortified lines

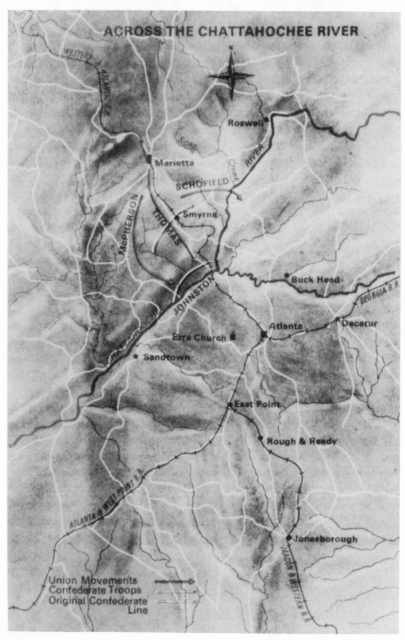

MAP 3.

around Smyrna, a small community a few miles south of Marietta on the railroad to Atlanta. These actions, fought on Independence Day, resulted in *Johnston's* being outflanked again. The next day the Confederate commander withdrew to the north bank of the Chattahoochee River, where a superb defensive line had been constructed ahead of time by impressed slave labor supervised by Confederate engineers. Here *Johnston* intended to hold Sherman at bay for a few days and then to withdraw over the river and into Atlanta's defensive works for the final round of the campaign.

Not wasting any time, Sherman began immediately to probe the river for suitable crossings. The Chattahoochee varies considerably as it runs north and west of Atlanta. There are wide shoals, deep portions, and narrow runs. The largest Union force, the Army of the Cumberland, held *Johnston* in place, while McPherson's army operated southward on the Confederates' left flank in order to create the illusion that the Chattahoochee might be crossed by the Federals in that direction. On July 5, Gen. Kenner Garrard's Union cavalry division seized and destroyed the small manufactories in the town of Roswell, on the Chattahoochee about twenty miles upstream from *Johnston's* position. Three days later, Schofield's army crossed the river about halfway between the Southern forces and Roswell, meeting only light opposition at Sope Creek, a small stream that empties into the river from the Cobb County (west) side. This maneuver successfully outflanked the Confederate river line, and *Johnston*, realizing that Atlanta was in danger of capture if he did not act quickly, hurriedly withdrew his troops to the Atlanta side of the Chattahoochee during the night of July 9-10. As they crossed the river, the Confederate forces destroyed the W&A railroad bridge and all other bridges within their lines. Beginning on July 8 and continuing for the next nine days, the Union forces crossed the Chattahoochee at several points on makeshift pontoon bridges. Thus Sherman's superbly executed series of flanking maneuvers brought him a much quicker victory at the Chattahoochee than was expected. In so doing, the last major river barrier on his march to Atlanta was overcome, and the Federals were only eight miles from the center of the city.

Most of Thomas's army crossed at Pace's and Power's Ferries, while McPherson's troops passed over the reconstructed road bridge at Roswell. Gen. Oliver O. Howard's 4th Corps of Thomas's army, however, was broken down into its constituent divisions for the purpose of protecting and assisting various other crossing efforts and thus crossed at two different locations. Once across, the Federals began to march south and southeast toward Atlanta and Decatur, a small town six miles east of Atlanta on the Georgia Railroad. Thomas occupied the area north of Peachtree Creek from near the point where it flowed into the Atlanta side of the Chattahoochee to the confluence of the creek's two forks about five miles directly east. After marching through Decatur, Schofield joined the left of Thomas and deployed in a line approximately three miles northeast of the center of Atlanta. Garrard's cavalry, with the aid of McPherson's infantry, seized Decatur and points east along the railroad to Stone Mountain, and together they destroyed the Georgia Railroad track between those two towns. Breaking this railroad severed Atlanta's rail connection eastward to Augusta, the Carolinas, and Virginia and prevented possible reinforcements from General *Lee's* army. After his work of destruction was done, McPherson closed in on Atlanta and connected to Schofield's left. Thus the Federal lines now constituted a twelve-mile-long crescent that arched north and northeast of Atlanta about five to seven miles from the heart of the city.

With Atlanta threatened, an old personal feud between Gen. *Johnston* and Confederate Pres. *Jefferson Davis* broke out anew. Throughout the campaign, *Johnston* had taken neither *Davis* nor the president's military advisor, General *Bragg*, into his confidence concerning plans for defeating Sherman and defending Atlanta. But at least once during the long summer of hard fighting, *Johnston* did reveal his thoughts in detail. Earlier in the campaign, during the time that the Southern forces occupied the Kennesaw line, *Louis T. Wigfall*, a pro-Johnston Confederate senator, stopped in Marietta to discuss matters with *Johnston* while traveling from Richmond to Texas. In the presence of his trusted friend, *Johnston* revealed that he intended to look for opportunities to sally forth from prepared field fortifications to defeat Federal detachments one by one. If the Union army was still largely intact by the time he had withdrawn close to Atlanta, *Johnston* continued, he would attack and attempt to cripple Sherman's armies as they divided while crossing Peachtree Creek. Should this plan fail, *Johnston* intended to withdraw his army into Atlanta's defensive perimeter and use the Georgia Militia to hold the face of these works, while the Army of Tennessee looked for further opportunities to defeat the enemy. Finally, the Confederate commander believed Southern cavalry forces in the Western Theater should be dispatched to break Sherman's long and vulnerable railroad supply line.

Later in the campaign the arrival of General *Bragg*, whom *Johnston* had replaced as commander of the Army of Tennessee and from whom he could expect trouble, signaled further displeasure from Richmond. On the morning of July 17, as he conferred with Col. *Stephen W. Presstman,* his chief engineer, *Johnston* received an unexpected and disappointing telegram from the Confederate army's adjutant and inspector general, *Samuel Cooper:*

> Lieutenant General *J.B. Hood* has been commissioned to the temporary rank of General under the late law of Congress. I am directed by the Secretary of War to inform you that as you have failed to arrest the advance of the enemy to the vicinity of Atlanta, far in the interior of Georgia, and express no confidence that you can defeat or repel him, you are hereby re-

Also symbolic of another role Atlanta played during the Civil War is this view of the Potter House, with its yard carved into trenches and artillery forts and its outbuildings and trees rendered into supports for the fortifications. (LC)

lieved from the command of the Army and Department of Tennessee, which you will immediately turn over to General *Hood.*

Having been dismissed from command and not reassigned, *Johnston* traveled to Macon, from whence he would follow the fortunes of his former army under its new leader. From this point on, a new offensive attitude would direct the actions of the Confederate forces defending Atlanta.

By the summer of 1864, the thirty-three-year-old *John Bell Hood* was only a remnant of the fine physical specimen he had been when the war began. Wounds received in the Battles of Gettysburg and Chickamauga had cost *Hood* the use of his left arm and had resulted in the amputation of his right leg. There is evidence that *Hood* was taking the opiate laudanum to relieve the pain of his wounds and that the drug may have impaired his judgment.

Hood spent the first two days of his command formulating a strategy for defeating Sherman. Ironically, he decided on a basic plan very similar to *Johnston's:* he would hold the lines around the city but would venture out to attack Union forces when he saw a chance. The differences between *Johnston* and *Hood* were more in temperament than in strategy. By nature, *Johnston* was cool and thoughtful, whereas *Hood* was an impetuous fighter who could be counted on to attack Sherman often.

Sherman, of course, had his own plans. He was determined to avoid costly frontal assaults on Atlanta's strong fortifications. A dispatch to Washington on July 6 revealed Sherman's intentions: "instead of attacking Atlanta direct, or any of its forts, I propose to make a circuit, destroying all its railroads. This is a delicate movement and must be done with caution."

Thus in two-and-a-half months, Union forces had advanced from Chattanooga approximately a hundred miles down the Blue Ridge to cross the Chattahoochee River and be poised on the doorstep of Atlanta. The campaign had been costly for Sherman, who had lost nearly 15,500 troops as he engaged in flanking well-entrenched Confederate forces that systematically retreated. Sherman's one major frontal assault, Kennesaw Mountain, had been a failure. In the next six weeks, numerous encounters would take place before Southern forces finally abandoned the city. During this period there were dozens of raids and skirmishes, but four major battles stand out as the critical episodes of the Atlanta Campaign: Peachtree Creek, Atlanta, Ezra Church, and Jonesboro. (Map 4)

The Battle of Peachtree Creek:
Tour One

General Description of the Battle

Confederate Gen. *John Bell Hood* directed two of his corps commanders, Gen. *Alexander P. Stewart* and Gen. *William J. Hardee*, to entrench their troops about a mile and a half north of Atlanta's defensive works in a line running west to east for about six miles. *Hood's* old corps, now commanded by Gen. *Benjamin F. Cheatham*, had orders to hold the continuation of this line southward two miles to its terminus just north of the Georgia Railroad, which Garrard's and McPherson's Union forces had recently cut. *Hood* planned to attack Thomas's Army of the Cumberland as it crossed Peachtree Creek to the north of Atlanta, while *Cheatham's* assignment was to hold off Schofield's and McPherson's Union troops east of the city. *Hood* intended to push Thomas's men back into the Chattahoochee River, thus destroying the largest of Sherman's three armies. The attack was set for 1 P.M., July 20, early enough, *Hood* hoped, to catch Thomas's soldiers before they could entrench south of the creek.

Beginning on the eighteenth and continuing apace on the twentieth, many blue-clad soldiers were advancing toward Atlanta from the north and the east. Dawn of the twentieth revealed troops from the 14th, 20th, and portions of the 4th Corps (all part of the Army of the Cumberland) busily crossing to the Atlanta side of Peachtree Creek and fortifying their positions. Gen. John Newton's division of Howard's 4th Corps was posted behind hastily built barricades that began near the junction of Clear Creek and Peachtree Creek and extended west along the route of Brighton Road,* ending at the site now occupied by Piedmont Hospital on Peachtree Street. The rest of the 4th Corps was attached temporarily to Schofield's army about three-and-a-half miles to the east. Knowing from reconnaissance reports of this gap between portions of the 4th Corps, *Hood* made it one of his most important objectives in the impending battle. In addition, no Federal units were positioned from the right of Newton's line to Tanyard Branch, a small

---

* Present-day street and road names are used unless otherwise indicated. Most of these streets and roads, of course, did not exist at the time.

stream running north to Peachtree Creek. This created another, but smaller, undefended section of the line.

Other Union units completed the line westward to the Chattahoochee River. Two divisions of Gen. Joseph Hooker's 20th Corps crossed Peachtree Creek at Northside Drive and marched southward to high ground where they fortified their positions. Gen. John W. Geary's division was posted along Collier Road from Tanyard Branch to Howell Mill Road. Gen. Alpheus S. Williams's division was slightly behind Geary's, with its left near the intersection of Norfleet Road and Northside Drive and its right resting near the intersection of Howell Mill and Greenbrook Drive. Hooker's remaining division, that of Gen. William T. Ward, was still a few miles north across the creek. Gen. John M. Palmer's 14th Corps occupied the area south of Peachtree Creek from Howell Mill Road westward to the vicinity of the Chattahoochee River.

Hood ordered the Southern generals to begin the battle by attacking the gap between Newton's division and the rest of the 4th Corps. The assault was to start with the far right of *Hardee's* corps and proceed with each division advancing after the one to its right had gone into battle; thus the Federals were to be swept westward down the valley of Peachtree Creek to the river and there destroyed. Before the battle could be joined, word came from Gen. *Joseph Wheeler,* commander of the Confederate cavalry corps, that he was being pushed back toward Atlanta by Federal forces approaching from the east. *Hood* decided to postpone the attack while *Cheatham's* front was extended southward to stem the advance of McPherson, Schofield, and part of Howard. The delay, however, dragged on till 4 P.M. before the signal to advance at last was given to the anxious Confederates north of the city. (Map 5)

The line of works from which *Hood's* columns attacked began near Crestlawn Cemetery, approximately five miles northwest of the city, and ran eastward for almost six miles to the intersection of Highland Avenue and Zimmer Drive. There it turned south for nearly two miles to the junction of Cleburne Avenue and Highland Avenue. In line-of-battle outside the trenches and awaiting the start of the assault was Gen. *William B. Bate's* division of Hardee's corps on the right flank; the divisions of Gens. *William H. T. Walker* and *George Maney* were in the center and on the left, respectively. *Hardee* held Gen. *Patrick R. Cleburne's* elite division in the works in reserve on the far right, to be committed at just the right moment to tip the scales in favor of the Confederates. To *Hardee's* left was *Stewart's* corps, with the divisions of Gen. *William W. Loring* on the right, Gen. *Edward C. Walthall* in the center, and Gen. *Samuel G. French* in the fortifications in reserve on the far left of the Confederate line.

At approximately 4 P.M., the battle started. *Hood's* Confederates emerged from their works and began the attack by advancing their right flank. *Bate's* men, moving through dense thickets along Clear

Creek, encountered no initial resistance. Finally they ran into Newton's left, where a hastily assembled group of Union infantry and artillery halted the attackers. *Walker's* Confederate division, the next to advance, struck the part of Newton's division that lay astride Peachtree Street. The Confederates overlapped a portion of Newton's right, for a time posing a great threat until Newton realigned the right of his division in an attempt to thwart the Southern advance. *Maney's* Confederate infantry rushed into the space between Newton and Geary and continued until they clashed with Ward's division, which had just crossed Peachtree Creek and was counterattacking.

Meanwhile, *Stewart's* troops had also moved to the attack. *Loring's* Confederate division swept forward and overran the 33rd New Jersey Infantry, which was posted on a high hill in Geary's front so that it could warn of Confederate attacks. *Loring's* right ran into Ward's troops as the latter were driving *Maney* back near Collier's Mill on Tanyard Branch. The left of *Loring's* line and *Walthall's* Confederate division struck Geary's center and right and forced the Federals to retreat hastily to the vicinity of the Bitsy Grant Tennis Center, where Geary's troops joined with the left of Williams's Union division. Excited by the retreat of the Federals in their front, *Walthall's* troops rushed headlong into a deep ravine in Williams's and Geary's front, hoping to drive their Northern opponents back into Peachtree Creek but meeting instead a storm of artillery and infantry fire which brought the Southern attack to a halt.

All along the line for two hours, attacks were stubbornly launched by the Confederates and equally stubbornly resisted by the Federals. By 6 P.M., most of the energy of the Southern assaults on Thomas had been expended. Just as *Hardee* was deciding to renew the attack and put *Cleburne's* reserve division in line-of-battle, a message from *Hood* arrived ordering *Hardee* to send a division to the east side of the city to reinforce the hard-pressed Confederates there. *Cleburne's* fresh troops were chosen for the task, and their departure ended any hope of continuing the attack along Peachtree Creek. By nightfall, all the surviving Confederates had withdrawn into their entrenchments, and *Hood's* first attempt to defeat a major portion of Sherman's forces had ended in failure.

It was a costly afternoon and evening: the Confederates suffered nearly 1,000 more casualties than the Federals. Of the 18,832 Southerners who participated in the Battle of Peachtree Creek, 2,500 were killed or wounded. The Federals, on the other hand, lost only 1,600 of the 20,139 engaged. After the battle, a conflict over responsibility for the defeat broke out between *Hood* and *Hardee*. *Hood* maintained that *Hardee* had not pressed the attack vigorously enough, while *Hardee* blamed *Hood* for removing the reserves just as they were about to be committed to the assault. The argument was never resolved, but it

is more likely that a combination of rough terrain, Federal entrenchments, and enfilading Union fire caused the Southern defeat. Possibly
equally important was the fact that *Hood* was not present at the battle
during its entire course—a failure of command that the Confederate
leader would repeat throughout the major battles around Atlanta. As
Southern commander, *Hood* did not need to lead his men from the very
front line, but he should have been on the Peachtree Creek Battlefield
all day to make the command decisions that were his responsibility.
Perhaps *Hood's* two previous wounds suffered in the thick of battle had
made him a bit timid about venturing directly into the fray. More important than this squabble among the Confederate high command or
Hood's conceivable personal timidity was the menace posed to Atlanta
by the Federal advance from the east. *Hood*, consequently, soon turned
his thoughts to devising a plan to defeat McPherson and Schofield.

The Driving Tour of the Peachtree Creek Battlefield
(approximately 15 miles)

Begin the tour from downtown at Central City Park near the point where early railroads came together to form the heart of the city—known today as Five Points. (Map 6) As you drive north on Peachtree Street, remember that you are in a metropolitan area of over two million people, one that is commonly regarded as the hub of the South. When the Civil War began in 1861, Atlanta was a small but bustling railroad town of about 7,000 people. By 1864, the city had become vitally important to the Confederacy. The city's population had swollen to 20,000, and industrial facilities capable of manufacturing artillery, armor plating for naval vessels, small arms, railroad materials, uniforms, and many other war items were located here.

Looking west along Peachtree Creek, the stream that lent its name to the famous battle on July 20, 1864, toward the Northside Drive bridge. Two divisions of Gen. Joseph Hooker's 20th Army Corps, those of Gens. John W. Geary and Alpheus S. Williams, crossed the creek on the nineteenth and twentieth on improvised bridges erected by some of Geary's men and located in the vicinity of the present-day bridge. Geary's and Williams's Federals seized a ridge beyond the left of the photograph and were later assaulted during the battle by two divisions of Gen. *Alexander P. Stewart's* Confederate corps. (All present-day photographs were made by Atlanta Historical Society staff photographer William Fullmer Hull, unless otherwise noted.)

When you cross North Avenue and Ponce de Leon Avenue near the Fox Theater, you will have reached the northern limits of the 1864 city and will have passed through the site of a portion of the earthen fortifications built to protect Atlanta from Sherman's armies. *Lemuel P. Grant*, a local resident who had been an engineer for the Georgia Railroad, directed the construction of the fortifications, which were still unfinished by mid-July of 1864. When General *Hood* assumed command of the Army of Tennessee on July 17, he ordered Colonel *Presstman*, his chief engineer, to complete the work on the defensive lines so that they could be used effectively if needed.

About 3 miles from the center of the city, near where Beverly Road intersects Peachtree Street close to the WSB-TV station, you will pass through the outer line of fortifications from which *Hardee's* and *Stewart's* Confederates assaulted the Union lines on July 20.

Continue north on Peachtree Street for another 1.5 miles. As you drive across the bridge over Peachtree Creek, you will be near the area where the Union forces of Wood's division of the 4th Corps and Ward's 20th Corps division crossed the creek heading south toward Atlanta.

Just past Peachtree Creek, take the first left onto Peachtree Battle Avenue. (Be careful, because this is a double intersection, and you must take the road farthest north.) You are now traveling west; several hundred yards south, on your left, is Peachtree Creek, the sluggish stream which gave this battle its name. In approximately 1.2 miles, Peachtree Battle intersects Northside Drive. Turn left.

You will pass over Peachtree Creek at precisely the same place that Geary's and Williams's divisions of the 20th Corps crossed on July 19 and 20, 1864. Once you have reached the top of the hill and have started down again (about .5 miles south of the creek), turn right onto Norfleet Road, a pleasant wooded avenue.

After about .3 miles, Norfleet intersects Howell Mill Road. (It is a tricky intersection because McKinley Road also ends here.) Make a left turn onto Howell Mill Road, go one block, and turn left on Collier Road. Howell Mill Road marks the farthest westward extent of that portion of the Union line that was directly assaulted during the Battle of Peachtree Creek. On your left all along the portion of Collier Road that you travel for about 1.2 miles back to Peachtree Street was the line held by Geary's and eventually Ward's divisions of the 20th Corps.

At Peachtree Street turn left, go one block, and turn right on Brighton Road. The ground on which Piedmont Hospital now stands was occupied by the right brigade of Newton's 4th Corps division. This unit was detached from the rest of its parent corps and put under the direct command of General Thomas, who was in overall command of the Union forces at Peachtree Creek.

Follow Brighton, bearing off to the left. You are now in Brookwood Hills, one of Atlanta's most attractive neighborhoods. This road runs along the crest of the ridge occupied by the remainder of Newton's divi-

Looking north along Wakefield Drive from its intersection with Camden Road toward the point where Wakefield and Brighton Road intersect uphill and in the distance. The area included in this photograph lies within the Brookwood Hills neighborhood. The high ridge running left to right in the distance forms part of the ground upon which Federal Gen. John Newton's 4th Corps division, which faced downhill toward the foreground, was assaulted by Gens. *William H. T. Walker's* and *William B. Bate's* divisions of Gen. *William J. Hardee's* Confederate corps. This action opened the Battle of Peachtree Creek at approximately 4 P.M. on July 20 and ended in the repulse of the Confederates.

Looking northwest across Peachtree Street toward Piedmont Hospital. A stone monument commemorating that Battle of Peachtree Creek is near the left edge of the photograph. The westward continuation (from right to left) of Newton's division of the 4th Corps crossed the road and ended on the hospital site. The right flank of Newton's Federals faced toward the left of the photograph and was attacked from that direction by portions of Gens. *William H. T. Walker's* and *George Maney's* divisions, both of *Hardee's* Confederate corps. Newton's position was greatly endangered by its Southern assailants, who were eventually driven back southward to the left.

Looking west along Collier Road toward Tanyard Creek Park, also the Memorial Site of the Battle of Peachtree Creek. Andrew J. Collier's mill stood within the boundaries of the park. Gen. John W. Geary's 20th Corps division was positioned on the high ground to the right (north) and faced the road. Repeatedly stormed from the left by Gens. *William W. Loring's* and *Edward C. Walthall's* divisions of Gen. *Alexander P. Stewart's* Confederate corps during the course of the battle, most of Geary's Federals were forced to withdraw northward to a more secure position. The portion that did not withdraw was located along this part of Collier. Numerous historical plaques in the vicinity of the park relate more of the details of the fighting in this area.

sion. As you round a large curve at the end of Brighton Road, you may look to the left in the direction of Clear Creek, which was the eastern boundary of the Federal forces fighting at Peachtree Creek. When you complete the curve, you will be on Camden Road. To your right, up the slope, charged the Confederates of *Bate's* and *Walker's* divisions to begin the Battle of Peachtree Creek. Opposing the Southerners, Newton's Federals were outflanked on both the right and left of their division. Reserve artillery, personally positioned and directed by General Thomas on the north side of Peachtree Creek, poured a steady fire into *Bate's* men who were struggling through the thickets along Clear Creek. On Newton's right, by Piedmont Hospital, the readjustment of part of the line and the timely arrival of Ward's 20th Corps division prevented *Maney's* Confederates from seizing an undefended segment of Thomas's Federal line.

Continue on Camden Road until it ends at Montclair Road. Turn right onto Montclair and return to Brighton Road. Bear left back onto Brighton (being sure to stay on the right side of the median) and travel

Looking south along Northside Drive in the vicinity of the Bitsy Grant Tennis Center toward a high, step ridge atop which Collier Road runs from left to right. The high ground on the right marks the left flank of General Williams's division of Hooker's corps. The ridge in the distance was occupied by General Geary's division of the same corps and followed the course of Collier Road from Tanyard Creek Park to Howell Mill Road. During the Battle of Peachtree Creek, Gen. *Edward C. Walthall's* division of Gen. *Alexander P. Stewart's* Confederate corps turned Geary's right flank near Howell Mill Road and forced most of these Federals to retreat down the ridge in the center of the photograph, toward the foreground. Approximately at the entrance of the tennis center (on the left), Geary's troops joined those of Williams. Thinking they would overrun the Union position in this area, *Walthall's* Confederates rushed down the ridge but were met and repulsed by Williams's and Geary's Federals.

to its intersection with Peachtree Street. Turn left on Peachtree, travel back to Collier Road, and turn right. As you drive westward, you are once again in the midst of the area that witnessed the heaviest fighting at Peachtree Creek. From your left to your right charged the Confederate divisions of *Walker, Maney,* and *Loring.* On your right, they clashed with the Federal divisions of Newton, Ward, and Geary.

About .6 miles from the intersection of Peachtree Street and Collier Road, you will come to Tanyard Branch Park on your left. Park your car in the small parking lot and walk down to the open field where two small streams flow together. This park was completed during the centennial celebration of the Civil War to commemorate the Battle of Peachtree Creek. Look toward the high ground opposite Collier Road, and you will be facing the direction from which *Loring's* and *Walthall's* divisions of *Stewart's* Confederate corps attacked. *Loring's* men passed over the ground on which you are standing and attacked Geary's Union division, which was partially entrenched on the other side of Collier Road. As you look toward the automobile bridge over Tanyard Branch, you will be facing the position occupied by Ward's 20th Corps division, which had to push back parts of *Loring's* and *Maney's* Confederate divisions when they rushed into the gap between Newton and Geary. The fighting in this vicinity was particularly heavy around the mill built by Andrew J. Collier, one of this area's first settlers. To the west, toward Howell Mill Road, *Walthall's* troops attacked the right flank of Geary's line, which ended near the intersection of Collier Road and Howell Mill Road. This flank was in advance (south) of Williams's deployed line to the west of Northside Drive.

When leaving the park, go directly across Collier to Overbrook Drive. When this road runs into Northside Drive, turn right and then quickly turn right again into the Bitsy Grant Tennis Center. Park your car and walk back to the entrance. Face southward along Northside Drive and look toward Overbrook Drive. On the ridge in front of you, Geary's division was posted, and on the ridge to your immediate right (the continuation of the one you are standing on), Williams's division was positioned. When *Walthall's* Confederates attacked Geary's exposed right, the center and right brigades of his Union division retreated hastily down the slope in front of you and joined Williams's left, at the spot where you now stand. Into the ravine in front of you and along which Norfleet Road runs, plunged *Walthall's* eager Confederate infantry. They were literally cut to pieces by the steady fire from the infantry and artillery of Williams's and Geary's Union troops.

All along the battlefield that you have traversed, the Confederate attacks were halted by the seasoned veterans of General Thomas's Army of the Cumberland. With the onset of nightfall, the Confederate commanders ordered their weary divisions to withdraw, and the Battle of Peachtree Creek came to an end. General *Hood's* first attempt to thwart the relentless advance of Sherman's armies toward Atlanta had ended in failure.

This brings to an end the tour of the Peachtree Creek Battlefield. To reach downtown for the second tour, turn left onto Northside Drive and continue until it intersects Marietta Street. This intersection marks the approximate area where Atlanta Mayor James M. Calhoun surrendered the city to elements of the Federal 20th Corps on September 2. For details on this episode, see pages 83-84. Turn left onto Marietta Street and follow it to Five Points.

The Battle of Atlanta:
Tour Two

General Description of the Battle

Sometimes the whole Atlanta Campaign is broadly referred to as the Battle of Atlanta, but in official histories the term Battle of Atlanta usually refers to the specific clash that occurred east of the city on July 22, the battle portrayed by the famous Cyclorama. At about the same time as the Battle of Peachtree Creek, McPherson's Army of the Tennessee, composed of the 15th, 16th, and 17th Corps, approached Atlanta from the general direction of Decatur, advancing along the course of the Georgia Railroad. Gen. John A. Logan's 15th Corps and Gen. Grenville M. Dodge's 16th Corps marched north of the railroad, while Gen. Frank P. Blair's 17th Corps proceeded south of the tracks. By this movement, McPherson hoped to capture the city, but sizable Confederate forces were deployed to stop his approach.

Gen. *Joseph Wheeler's* Confederate cavalry corps, fighting dismounted for the most part, and portions of Gen. *Benjamin F. Cheatham's* corps resisted McPherson's Federals. Gen. *Patrick R. Cleburne's* division was withdrawn from the Peachtree Creek area by *Hood* and hastily marched to the east side of Atlanta, where it reinforced *Wheeler's* troopers on an eminence known as Bald Hill, an important element in *Hood's* outer defensive line.

On the evening of July 21, McPherson's army was deployed with the 15th Corps astride the Georgia Railroad facing west toward Atlanta and with its right joining Schofield's 23rd Corps. The 17th Corps, which was connected to the left of the 15th Corps, opposed *Cleburne's* entrenched Confederate division on Bald Hill. That evening Gen. Mortimer D. Leggett's and Gen. Giles A. Smith's divisions of Blair's 17th Corps took Bald Hill, which forced *Hood* to abandon the portion of his outer defensive line that faced the Union forces of Logan and Blair. During the previous few days, as McPherson's troops had advanced toward Atlanta in a large half-circle from the east, their lines had contracted as they neared the city, thus displacing General Dodge's 16th Corps, which pulled out of the Army of the Tennessee's line and formed a reserve contingent in the rear of the army.

Upon hearing that Bald Hill had fallen, thus putting the city in im-

29

minent danger of close-range bombardment, *Hood* decided to launch a grand flank attack on McPherson, whose troops formed the extreme left of Sherman's forces. *Hood's* plan, which was largely an embellishment of *Johnston's* strategy, called for a withdrawal from the entire outer line to mask a flanking march to the south by *Hardee*, who was then to wheel around and fall upon the rear of McPherson, thereby destroying his Army of the Tennessee. Simultaneous with *Hardee's* attack, *Wheeler's* Confederate cavalry was to wreck McPherson's supply wagons gathered at Decatur. The rest of *Hood's* army was detailed to hold the inner defensive line, a ten-mile circuit of heavily reinforced trenches and artillery forts, which protected Atlanta itself. The plan also called for the Confederates within the city's fortifications to join the attack at the decisive moment and sweep all the Federals back to Peachtree Creek; this was yet another example of *Hood's* grandiose and unworkable plans.

At midday on July 22, McPherson's Union army was deployed in a line running roughly north and south, facing west toward Atlanta. (Map 7) The three divisions of Logan's 15th Corps were on the north end of the line, which connected with Schofield's 23rd Corps. Gen. Charles R. Woods's division was positioned between North Highland Avenue and Euclid Avenue. Gen. Morgan L. Smith's division connected with Woods's left and extended southward across DeKalb Avenue and the Georgia Railroad. The last division of the corps, Gen. William Harrow's, joined with M. L. Smith's left near the intersection of Hardee Street and Moreland Avenue and continued the line of the corps south toward Bald Hill, which was located where Moreland Avenue passes over Interstate 20. Blair's 17th Corps was in line south of Logan. General Leggett's division of that corps was positioned on Bald Hill, also known as Leggett's Hill after the division that occupied it. The 17th Corps line was continued by Gen. G. A. Smith's troops, who were dug in along Flat Shoals Avenue in a manner resembling a "dangling fish-hook bent eastward" and ending just north of Glenwood Avenue. Dodge's 16th Corps, forming McPherson's reserve, was sent to buttress the left of the army. At the moment of the attack, one brigade of Gen. Thomas W. Sweeny's division was deployed north to south along Clay Street, with an exposed salient point on the grounds of Murphy High School. The division's other brigade extended southwestward from the school, roughly parallel to Memorial Drive, in the direction of G. A. Smith's 17th Corps division. One brigade of Gen. John W. Fuller's division, the remaining brigade of which was guarding the supply wagons at Decatur, joined with Sweeny's right. There was, however, between the 16th and 17th Corps a sizable gap which would play an important part in the impending battle.

Hardee's Confederate corps began withdrawing from its positions north and east of Atlanta early in the evening of July 21. McPherson's

Union forces became vaguely aware of *Hardee's* movements and were surprised by *Hood's* boldness only two days after his defeat at Peachtree Creek. By midnight the corps was out of the city and marching south on the McDonough Road. The goal was to get to the rear of McPherson's Federals, and the route was a fifteen-mile journey along twisting country lanes. By daylight on July 22, *Hardee* was still miles south of his objective and was not yet able to launch the dawn attack that *Hood* had ordered. Relying on the help of two local residents (William Cobb, the owner of a nearby mill, and his miller, Case Turner), *Hardee* was finally able to complete his flanking march through rough and heavily wooded terrain. By about noon his corps was deployed for battle. Because Garrard's Union cavalry division was away to the east on a raid at Covington, the approach of the Confederates upon McPherson's left flank went largely undetected. *Wheeler's* Confederate troopers concluded their ride eastward and deployed south of Decatur in preparation for the attack upon the Union supply wagons located there.

Hardee had been ordered to attack McPherson entirely from behind, but the difficulties encountered during his night march precluded such an assault. Gen. *William B. Bate's* troops were on the far right facing northwest. They stretched from the intersection of I-20 and Glenwood Avenue on the south to Memorial Drive on the north. Gen. *William H. T. Walker's* division joined *Bate's* left and extended the line south of Glenwood. Gen. *Patrick R. Cleburne's* men faced in the same direction as *Walker* and *Bate* but were forward of them and astride Flat Shoals Avenue and Glenwood. The last of *Hardee's* divisions, *Maney's*, was west of *Cleburne*, straddling I-20 and Moreland Avenue and facing northeastward toward Leggett's and G. A. Smith's Federals. The three divisions of Gen. *Benjamin F. Cheatham's* corps were still in the inner defensive line, but later that afternoon they would participate in the battle. Gen. *Alexander P. Stewart's* corps remained in the city's defenses and was ordered to hold in place the Union formations it opposed so they could not reinforce McPherson's Federal forces.

Early on the morning of July 22, Federal skirmishers found the Confederate outer line of works abandoned and the inner circuit heavily defended. Sherman, when informed of the situation, decided to advance McPherson's left flank around to the south side of Atlanta in order to threaten the city from that direction.

Sometime between 12:15 and 1 P.M., as these plans were being implemented, *Bate's* and *Walker's* Confederate divisions started the attack. Unsupported, *Bate's* infantry struck Dodge's Union line. Well-placed artillery and the successful repositioning of portions of his infantry allowed Dodge to repulse *Bate's* assault. *Walker's* troops advanced into battle next, attacking Fuller's lone brigade and the right of Sweeny's division. Before his men reached the Union lines, *Walker* was shot and killed by enemy pickets near the northern tip of Terry's Mill Pond, an impounded stream about which *Walker* and *Bate* had deployed their divisions. Gen. *Hugh W. Mercer* assumed command in *Walker's* place, but again the Southerners were unable to penetrate the Union lines.

These initial attacks were heard by McPherson as he lunched with a group of staff and line officers, including Generals Blair and Logan, near the site of the Candler Park MARTA (Metropolitan Atlanta Rapid Transit Authority) station. After dispatching most of his aides with various orders, McPherson rode south in the general direction of the firing, accompanied by a few officers. This group stopped on a point of high ground near General Dodge's right and from this height observed the fighting along Sweeny's line. After hearing firing from the southwest, McPherson and his orderlies then rode in that direction down a country lane to warn Gen. G. A. Smith of the impending attack on his 17th Corps division. Suddenly, they came upon a portion of the Confederate line-of-battle, and the group was ordered to surrender. Ignoring his would-be captors' demands, McPherson waved his hat in salute and spurred his horse. A volley of musketry rang out from the Southerners, and the general fell from his horse. McPherson died within twenty minutes, but most of the officers who accompanied him got away. Upon the report of McPherson's death, General Logan assumed command of the Army of the Tennessee, and Gen. M. L. Smith took control of the 15th Corps.

The unsuccessful attacks by *Mercer* and *Bate* struck the 16th Corps. None of the Confederate commanders had expected to find so large a body of Union troops in such a position. Meanwhile, to the west *Cleburne* was about to launch his first assault, which would strike the gap between the 16th and 17th Corps.

Cleburne's Confederates broke through the angle on the left of G. A. Smith's line and poured into the gap. In a desperate attempt to preserve their position, Smith's Union infantry crossed to the opposite side of their trenches and poured an enfilading fire into *Cleburne's* exposed ranks. This action combined with the arrival of a reserve brigade (Col. Hugo Wangelin's) drawn from Woods's division of the 15th Corps forced *Cleburne* to withdraw his troops.

Between 1 and 2 P.M., after a brief interlude, the Confederates made another attempt to crush the entrenched Federals of the 17th Corps. Meanwhile, General Logan, now temporarily in command of McPherson's army, had ordered G. A. Smith to look for an opportune moment to withdraw his division to a line facing south, connecting at right angles with Leggett on the west and Wangelin on the east. Thus one unbroken and more easily defended Federal line would be formed. Before this movement could be executed, however, *Cleburne*, this time accompanied by *Maney's* division to the west, moved up for another attack. Their assaults on G. A. Smith's and Leggett's Union divisions,

(Continued on page 49.)

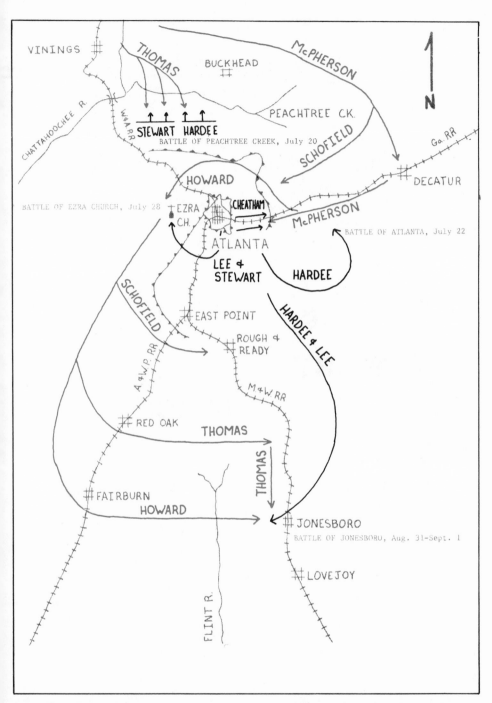

MAP 4. The four major battles around the Atlanta area: Peachtree Creek, Atlanta, Ezra Church, and Jonesboro. (Adapted from a map in *The Road Past Kennesaw*.)

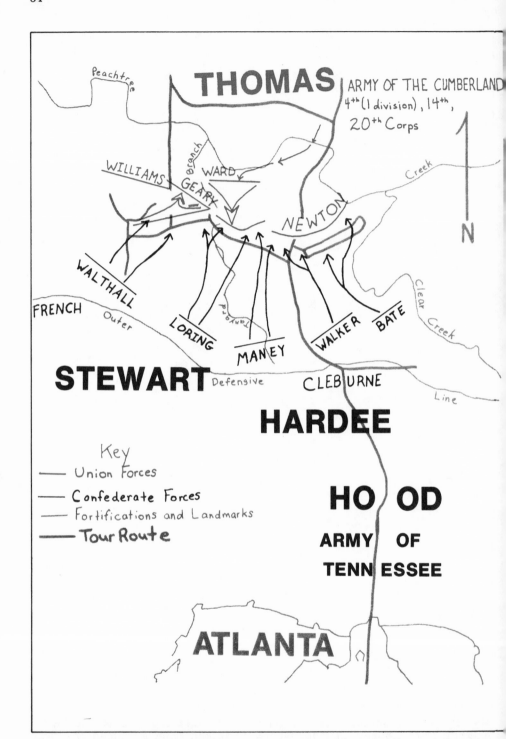

Map 5. The Battle of Peachtree Creek superimposed on present-day street map.

MAP 6. Route of the Battle of Peachtree Creek tour.

36

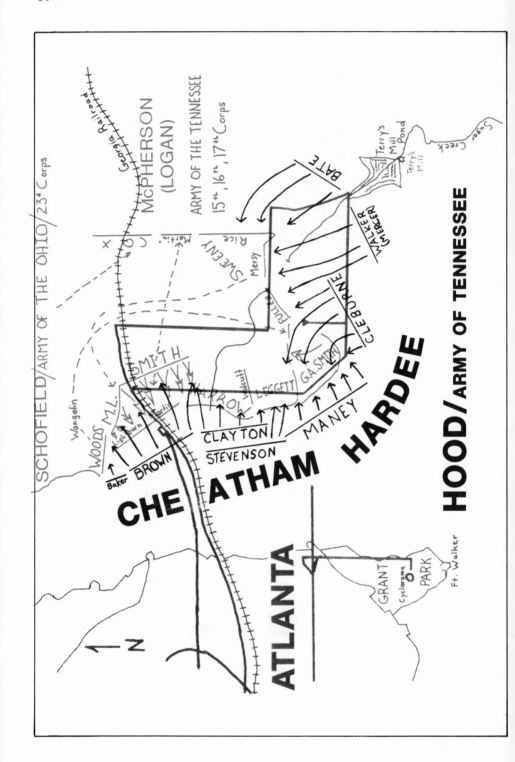

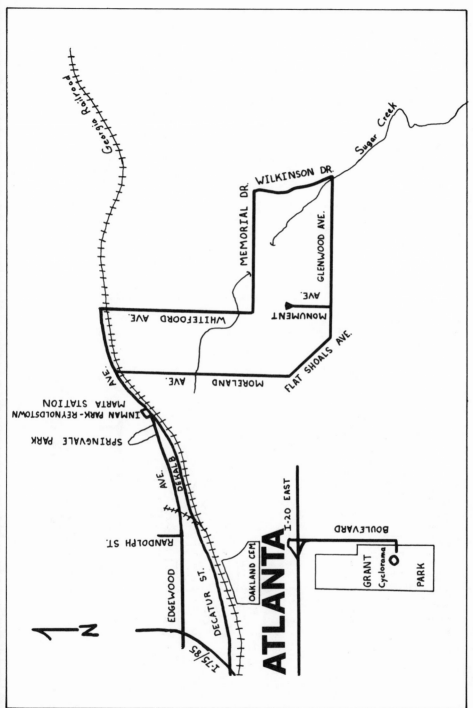

Map 8. Route of the Battle of Atlanta tour.

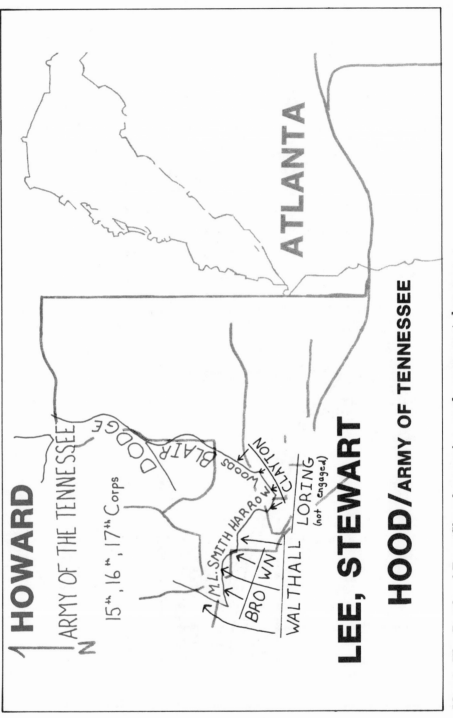

Map 9. The Battle of Ezra Church superimposed on present-day map.

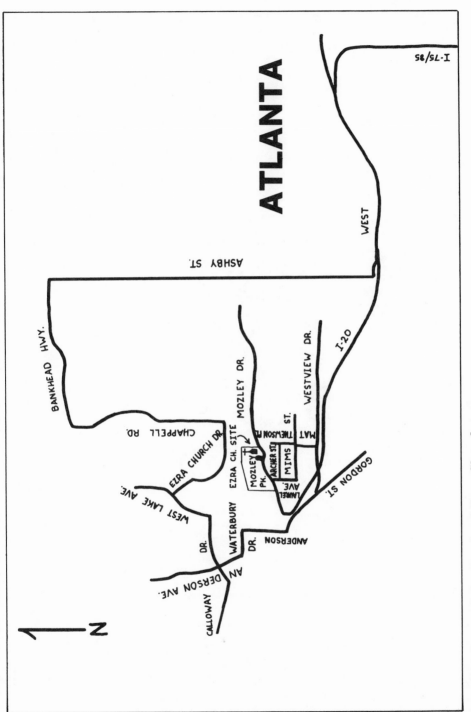

Map 10. Route of the Battle of Ezra Church tour.

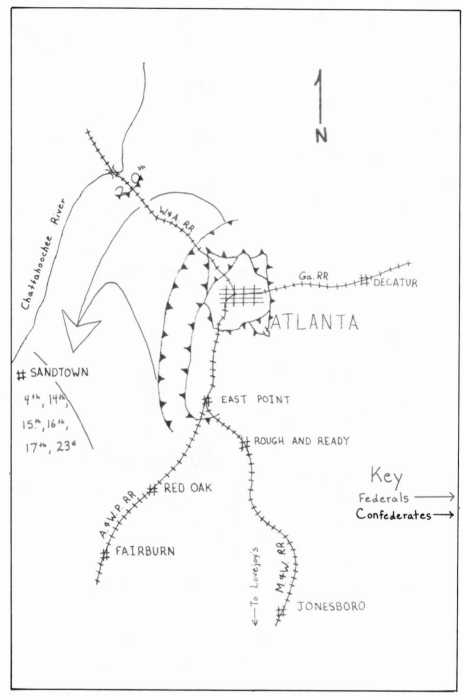

MAP 11. Movements of Sherman's armies, August 26.

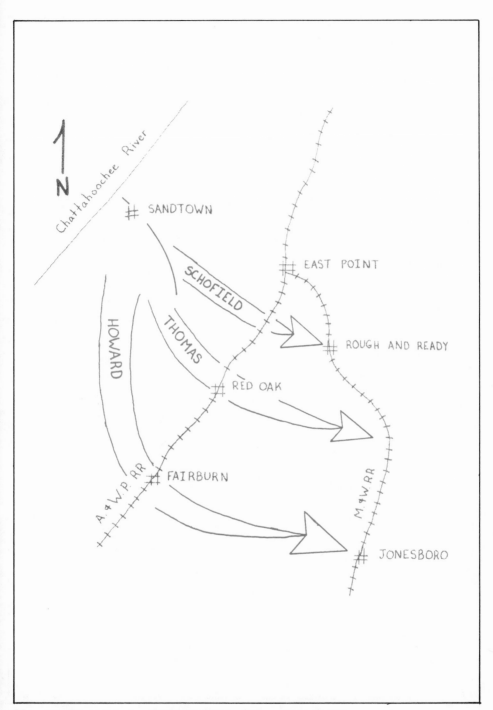

MAP 12. Movements of Sherman's armies, August 27.

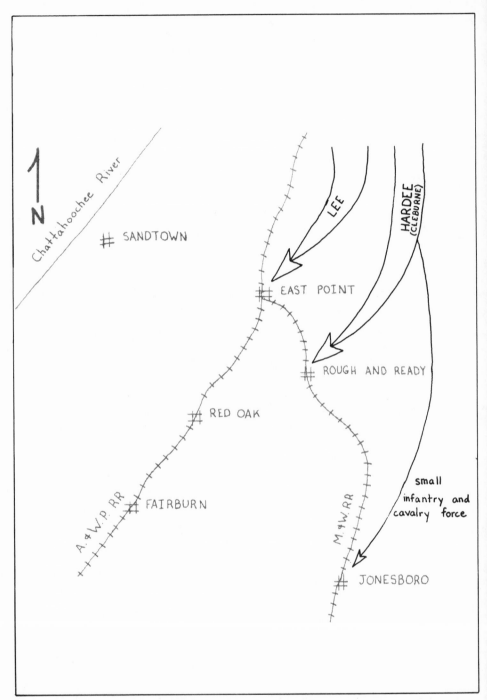

MAP 13. **Movements of Hoods' army, August 28.**

43

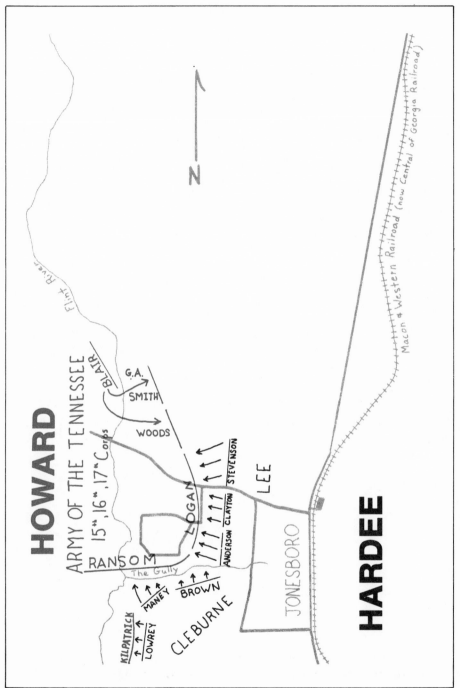

MAP 14. The Battle of Jonesboro (first day, August 31) superimposed on present-day road map.

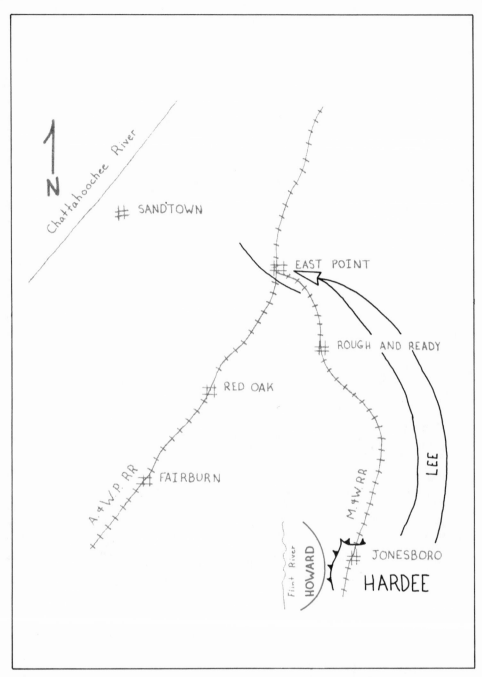

MAP 15. Movements of Hood's army, night of August 31-September 1.

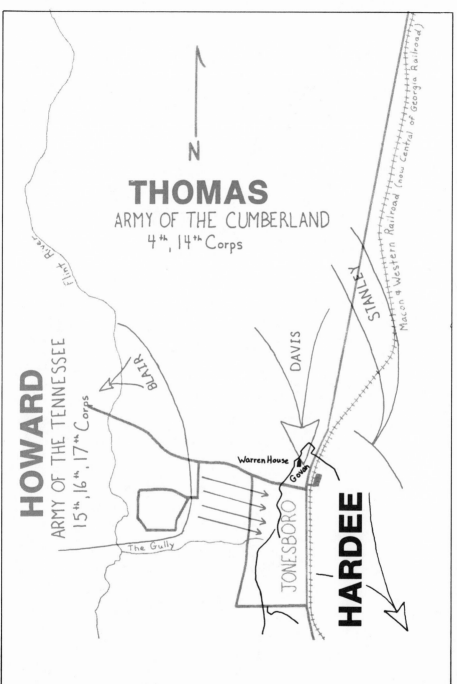

MAP 16. The Battle of Jonesboro (second day, September 1) superimposed on present-day map.

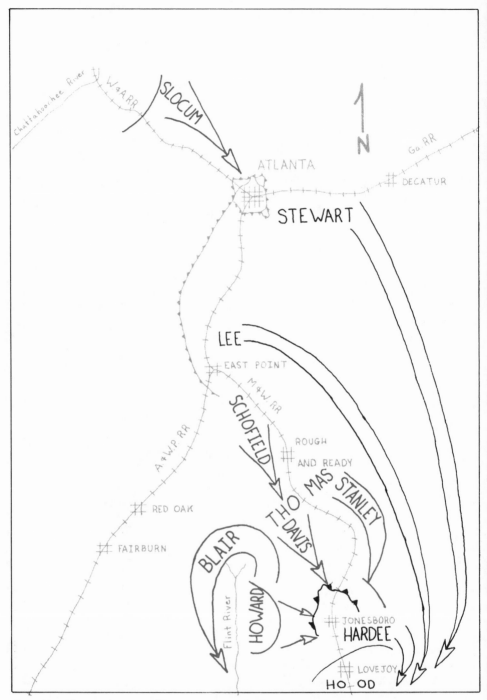

MAP 17. Movements of Sherman's and Hood's armies, September 1-2.

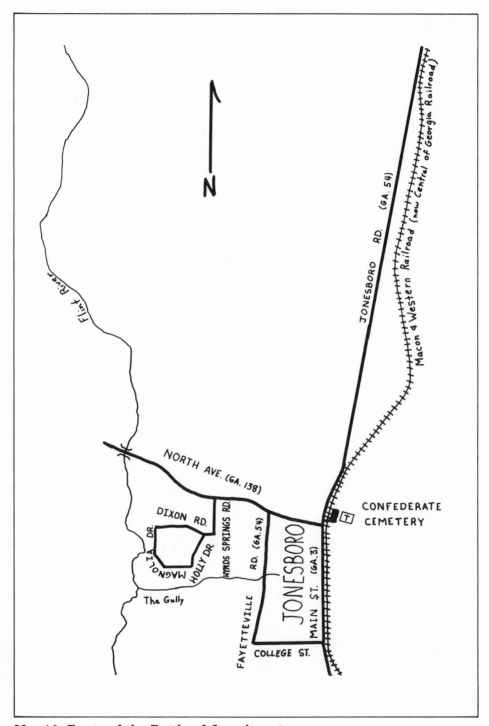

MAP 18. Route of the Battle of Jonesboro tour.

(Continued from page 32.)

Walcutt's brigade of Harrow's division, and Wangelin's 15th Corps reserve brigade were uncoordinated. For two hours the fighting between these units continued. G. A. Smith's and Leggett's infantry resisted Confederate attacks from both sides of their entrenchments, while Walcutt's and Wangelin's troops contributed to the repulse of *Cleburne's* forces.

Hood watched the battle from the second story of a house which stood within the present-day boundaries of Oakland Cemetery. Around 3 P.M., as *Hardee's* assaults were being turned back, *Hood* ordered General *Cheatham* to advance his corps against the 15th Corps as a diversion to assist *Hardee*. The departure of part of Col. James S. Martin's brigade of Morgan L. Smith's division to support the left of the 16th Corps had resulted in thinning the line of the 15th Corps just south of the Georgia Railroad. This thin interval in the Federal line was held by the balance of Martin's brigade and was bordered on the north by a deep cut through which ran the railroad to Augusta. North of the tracks, Gen. Joseph A. J. Lightburn's brigade continued the line of M. L. Smith's division. Martin's and Lightburn's sector was the focal point of some of the day's heaviest fighting.

Two divisions of *Cheatham's* corps were moved up and placed in line-of-battle. Gen. *John C. Brown's* division was deployed astride the Georgia Railroad, while Gen. *Henry D. Clayton's* division was aligned south of the tracks overlapping the right of *Brown*. Both of these Cohfederate units faced eastward toward M. L. Smith's and Harrow's divisions of the 15th Corps. Following a brief encounter with Federal pickets, *Clayton's* and *Brown's* infantry advanced on the Union works. They were met by heavy artillery and musketry fire and had to seek cover in a ravine about 400 yards from the Federal line. A portion of the ravine is extant in Springvale Park along Edgewood Avenue. The smoke produced by the heavy firing obscured the field of battle. Though the brigades of the two Confederate divisions were now intermingled, they advanced again, this time partially covered by the smoke. A portion of one Southern brigade burst through the railroad cut, which was the weakest point in the 15th Corps line. Surprised by the appearance of Confederate infantry in their midst, Lightburn's brigade and the remaining half of Martin's brigade, both from M. L. Smith's Union division, broke and ran. The immediate result was that the two Illinois batteries in the vicinity had to be abandoned to the enemy, since the artillerists were unable to remove their guns from the field. On the north end of the breakthrough, General Woods's division was forced to change the front of its left to face southward to keep from being outflanked. South of the hole in the line, the two right brigades of Harrow's Federal division, which connected with M. L. Smith's left, were now being assailed from front and rear. They, too, broke and withdrew eastward.

Logan ordered the return of M. L. Smith's detached brigade (Martin's) plus the transfer of one brigade from the 16th Corps to reinforce the threatened sector along the Georgia Railroad. General Sherman sent a message to Logan ordering him to counterattack and push the Confederates out of the gap they had seized. General Woods's infantry and six of his division's artillery pieces were to open fire on the Southern left. Meanwhile, from the left of Schofield's 23rd Corps, Sherman personally directed enfilading artillery fire that was intended to prevent any reinforcement of the Confederates attacking north of the railroad. M. L. Smith's division (now at full strength and assisted by Col. August Mersy's brigade from General Sweeny's division of the 16th Corps) and Harrow's two withdrawn brigades were ready to counterattack and push back the Confederates in their front. The counterstroke was launched, and the original Federal line was retaken amid close and desperate fighting. Capt. Francis De Gress, who commanded one of the captured Union batteries, advanced his artillerists with the infantry, and they were soon firing their recaptured guns at the retreating Southerners. By about 5 P.M., the attacks by *Clayton's* and *Brown's* Confederates had been repulsed.

At about the same hour, *Cleburne* and *Maney* renewed their attacks on the 17th Corps. By this time, the Confederates had already launched at least five assaults on Blair's Union corps, with the brunt of these charges being borne by Gen. G. A. Smith's hard-pressed Federal infantry and supporting artillery. The struggle along this portion of the line was some of the fiercest of the entire campaign. The sword and the bayonet were used freely by both sides as hand-to-hand fighting predominated. Around 7 P.M., G. A. Smith's troops withdrew in good order to a line perpendicular to Leggett's position, which had been proposed earlier in the day by General Logan. Once in place and joined to the 16th Corps by Wangelin's 15th Corps reserve brigade, the 17th Corps held off one last attempt by *Maney's* and *Cleburne's* infantry to storm the Union positions. By dark, the Army of the Tennessee was in one continuous line that could not be broken. The largest and costliest battle of the Atlanta Campaign had ended in yet another Confederate failure.

Off to the east at Decatur, *Wheeler's* Southern cavalry, fighting on foot, attacked the 16th Corps brigade assigned to protect the Army of the Tennessee's supply wagons. *Wheeler's* troopers greatly outnumbered their opponents and succeeded in driving the Federals north through Decatur. At this point, a group of staff officers from General *Hardee* arrived. They directed *Wheeler* to mount up his troopers and ride westward to assist *Hardee* in his last assault on the Federal lines in East Atlanta. As it turned out, *Wheeler's* assistance to *Hardee* was only minimal. When called away from Decatur, the Southern cavalrymen were pushing the Federals back toward the Union supply wagons, which were being withdrawn steadily northward in an attempt to keep them out of the reach of *Wheeler's* horsemen. An opportunity to wreck the supply vehicles of the Army of the Tennessee may have been lost.

The Battle of Atlanta was costly for both sides but especially for *Hood's* army. From a total of 36,934 who took part, the Southern forces suffered approximately 8,000 casualties. By contrast, although 30,477 Federal soldiers participated in the battle, there were only 3,722 casualties. Despite his losses, *Hood* tried to present the battle as a success. He claimed that the assault had stopped Sherman's attempt to envelop Atlanta from the east and south, and he maintained that the morale of his army had been uplifted by the battle. In fact, the events of July 22 did more to lessen the fighting spirit of *Hood's* troops than did any other event up to that point—except perhaps *Hood's* promotion to the army's command itself.

Hood blamed *Hardee* for the failure of the assaults on the Army of the Tennessee. He based his accusation on two points: the attack was launched too late in the day, and it was carried out in piecemeal fashion. Perhaps *Hardee* should not be held entirely responsible for the former, because the combination of a tiring night march, inept guides, and rough terrain covered by dense woods made it all but impossible for the intended daylight attack to take place. *Hardee*, on the other hand, committed his divisions individually throughout the day, so the charge about the piecemeal attack may have some validity. A concerted, coordinated assault on the Army of the Tennessee from its rear, as planned, might well have crippled one of Sherman's three armies beyond the point of being any longer an effective fighting force. Such a result could have made the effort to defend Atlanta more likely to succeed. As it was, *Hardee's* persistence in launching numerous assaults on fortified Union positions made *Hood's* task of defeating Sherman all the more difficult; however, the events two days earlier at Peachtree Creek and the ensuing altercation between *Hardee* and *Hood* over responsibility for that Confederate defeat may have caused *Hardee* to persist beyond the limits of reason in his attempt to gain a victory. In *Hardee's* defense, *Hood* was in overall command of the Southern forces defending Atlanta, and he should have been closer to the scene of the action than the house close in to the city from which he observed the battle. In short, *Hood* should have exercised the full privileges and responsibilities of being leader of the Confederate Army of Tennessee rather than passing battlefield command yet again to *Hardee*. Regardless of who caused the Southern defeat at the Battle of Atlanta, the preponderance of forces was now even more heavily weighted in Sherman's favor, and his union armies would soon make yet another attempt to close the ring around the Gate City of the South.

In contrast to the Confederate conduct of the battle, Sherman's generals managed their forces rather well. The sporadic fighting east of Atlanta during the two days prior to the major battle caused McPherson's three corps to become somewhat intermingled. Thus on the morning of July 22, McPherson was attempting several movements at once. He was extending his line southward and moving it generally westward in an attempt to wrap around the south side of Atlanta. Simultaneously, he was moving troops to cover the rear of the Army of the Tennessee, since an attack from that direction was suspected. He also planned to destroy the Georgia Railroad from the Union front line back eastward to the town of Decatur.

The Confederate attack, though late and not entirely unanticipated by McPherson and some of his subordinates, did take the Army of the Tennessee somewhat unaware. Cavalry often acted as the "eyes" of the army for both sides, so the absence of Garrard's Union troopers, who were raiding Covington, deprived McPherson and his commanders of much-needed detailed knowledge of Confederate movements. Though disaster could have been the result at this point, it was averted for several reasons. For one, after a good deal of repositioning of various units, the Army of the Tennessee's position came to resemble the shape of a box. Within the box, units could be moved around to reinforce portions of the line threatened by direct Confederate attacks. For example, Colonel Wangelin's reserve brigade of the 15th Corps was used effectively in holding back *Cleburne's* Confederate division from overrunning too much of the position held by the 17th Corps. Use of troops in this manner is called the principle of interior lines, or the use of the inner avenues of a closed (or nearly closed) defensive position to allow the rapid movement of reinforcements. Thus the free exchange of brigades by the divisions of the Army of the Tennessee is a credit to that army's unity and camaraderie. And last, the presence of much artillery and its effective use also contributed to the Federal victory at the Battle of Atlanta.

The Driving Tour of the Atlanta Battlefield
(approximately 10.6 miles)

Leave the Five Points area on Decatur Street and travel east toward Decatur. (Map 8) Decatur Street parallels the route of the Georgia Railroad, which extends east from Atlanta to Augusta. It also runs alongside the MARTA rapid rail line. (Be careful, because there are several turn-only and restricted lanes.) About a mile from Five Points, Oakland Cemetery will be on your right, just across the railroad tracks to the south. Oakland is Atlanta's oldest burial ground and was known as Atlanta or City Cemetery until 1876. It was relocated to its present site on June 6, 1850, and its size in 1864 was approximately one-third its current eighty-five acres. The site of the house from which General *Hood* watched the Battle of Atlanta is now within the cemetery. Just across the cemetery is the now closed Fulton Bag and Cotton Mill, established in 1881. A rolling mill which produced iron plating for Confederate naval vessels was located on the site of the mill.

About 1.5 miles from Five Points, as you drive over a set of railroad tracks in the street, Decatur Street becomes DeKalb Avenue. Continue eastward for 1 more mile, and the Inman Park-Reynoldstown MARTA station will be on your right. The entrenched line of the 15th Corps on July 22 crossed the Georgia Railroad near here.

Proceed on DeKalb Avenue for another .7 miles to the Candler Park station. Turn right onto Whitefoord Avenue. After you pass under the railroad tracks and start uphill, you will be on the high ground where General McPherson was taking lunch with two of his corps commanders and a group of staff officers when he heard the firing to the southeast (off to your left) that signaled the start of the Battle of Atlanta. As you drive south on Whitefoord Avenue, you will be approximating the route that led McPherson to his death at the hands of skirmishers from *Cleburne's* Confederate division. About 1 mile south of DeKalb Avenue, Whitefoord ends at Memorial Drive where you will turn left. On your immediate right is a hill upon which is Walker Memorial Park. From this height, McPherson saw *Bate's* and *Walker's* Confederate divisions as they attacked Dodge's 16th Corps in the initial assaults of the battle. McPherson rode south (to your right) from this hill toward the point at which he was killed, which is ahead on the tour.

As you continue on Memorial, you will be driving along that portion of the 16th Corps line that faced southward in the direction of the Confederate attackers. About .7 miles east from Walker Park is Murphy

53

Looking southeast across Memorial Drive toward Murphy High School. On July 22, 1864, the Battle of Atlanta began in this area as Union Gen. Thomas W. Sweeny's 16th Corps division and the 14th Battery, Ohio Light Artillery, defended the school site and surrounding areas against attacks from the opposite side of Murphy High by Gens. *William B. Bate's* and *William H. T. Walker's* divisions of Gen. *William J. Hardee's* Confederate corps.

Looking southeast along Wilkinson Drive toward its intersection with Glenwood Avenue. On the traffic island in the center of the photograph stands the monument locating the approximate site of the death of Gen. *William H. T. Walker*, a division commander in General *Hardee's* Confederate corps. The monument originally stood about a half mile west (right) but was later moved to its present site to bring the location of *Walker's* death in line with subsequent research.

High School. (This is a significant site, so you may want to stop near the school.) On the school grounds, Dodge's line formed a right angle. The corps extended west from the school along Memorial Drive toward Atlanta. This section was initially held by Colonel Mersy's brigade of Sweeny's 16th Corps division, which was joined on its right by Colonel Morrill's brigade from General Fuller's division of the same corps. From Murphy High, General Sweeny's other brigade, that of General Elliott W. Rice, ran north along Clay Street, which is directly across from the school on the north side of Memorial Drive. The apex of the angle was on the grounds of the school itself. This position was held not only by Sweeny's Federal infantry but also by the 14th Ohio Battery. The Battle of Atlanta began in this vicinity as *Bate's* Confederate division attacked from the southeast. It was this fighting that McPherson observed just before riding to his death.

Just past Murphy High School turn right on Wilkinson Drive, which more or less traces the path of attack toward the Murphy High site by *Bate's* division of Confederates. On your left at the intersection of Wilkinson and Glenwood Avenue is a monument erected to mark the approximate location of the death of Gen. *W.H.T. Walker*, a Confederate who was killed by Federal pickets as he deployed his division in line-of-battle.*

Turn right onto Glenwood Avenue. As you go west over I-20 and Sugar Creek, you will be at the northern tip of what was Terry's Mill Pond. (I-20 construction changed this area's topography considerably.) *Bate's* and *Walker's* divisions were deployed on opposite sides of this creek in preparation for their assaults on the Union lines to your right (north). Continue westward on Glenwood. After about .5 miles, you will enter the area traversed by General *Cleburne's* division as it advanced to the attack from your left to your right in its repeated attempts to defeat the Union formations in its front. The force of *Cleburne's* assaults was reduced by the swampiness of the ground and the thick undergrowth in this area, both of which broke up the alignment of the Confederates. The fighting here and to the north (your right) was desperate. Often Federals and Confederates used bayonets and swung their muskets like baseball bats. Two of *Cleburne's* three brigades lost about one-half their number in casualties during these attacks.

Approximately .7 miles from Wilkinson Road, turn right onto Monument Avenue. The monument at the end of the road marks the place where the young, promising General McPherson, who had topped his class at West Point, fell. Only thirty-five years old in 1864, he had risen to command a Union army and was one of Sherman's personal favor-

---

* The spot where the monument stands today is not its original location. The monument was unveiled on July 22, 1902, the thirty-eighth anniversary of the battle, about a half mile west of its present location. Subsequent research indicated that it had been misplaced, and thus it was moved to this spot in August 1936 so that its location would coincide with the later, more correct research.

Looking northwest toward the McPherson Monument at the northern terminus of Monument Avenue. Gen. James B. McPherson, commander of the Union Army of the Tennessee, was killed at this location early in the Battle of Atlanta by skirmishers from Confederate Gen. *James A. Smith's* Texas brigade.

ites. At the moment of his death, McPherson was accompanied by only a few officers. The shots that killed him were fired by soldiers of Gen. *James A. Smith's* brigade of General *Cleburne's* division. The horse ridden by a Signal Corps officer, Lieutenant William H. Sherfy, who was near McPherson, bolted at the sound of the shots and raced uncontrollably into the woods. Sherfy was knocked from his horse when he struck the limb of a tree, and the impact broke his watch. When he regained consciousness shortly thereafter and returned safely to the Union lines, his watch read 2:02 P.M., thus fixing the time of McPherson's death. The place where McPherson's body lay was overrun by Confederate soldiers. His remains were searched but nothing of importance was taken. Later in the day, Union forces recovered the general's body and most of his personal property.* Drive completely around the

* The version of McPherson's death given here is the result of combining several wartime and postwar accounts. Only the essential details have been included, and even these may be disputed by some sources. McPherson died in the midst of a campaign, so no one had time to set down the complete details of his death. Atlantan Bill Erquitt has evidence that McPherson may have followed a somewhat different route to this site. He argues that McPherson rode first to the vicinity of Murphy High School. From there, he heard firing off to the west in the direction of Gen. G. A. Smith's 17th Corps division. Perhaps because a ridge line, part of which today is Walker Park, obscured his direct observation of G. A. Smith's position, McPherson rode in that direction to check on the situation. After traveling a short distance along a road that had been used frequently during the day and was apparently safe, McPherson rode into a wood where he was shot by *Cleburne's* men. This theory deviates from the accepted interpretation only in the route taken by McPherson and not in the site of his death.

The site of Gen. James B. McPherson's death, July 22, 1864. (AHS)

monument and return on Monument Avenue to Glenwood Avenue. Turn right, go three blocks, and then turn right again onto Flat Shoals Avenue.

Flat Shoals follows a gently sloping ridge along which Giles A. Smith's 17th Corps division was entrenched. Smith's division bore the brunt of the Confederate attacks during the battle. Receiving no less than six direct assaults from their front, flank, and rear during the day, Smith's men repulsed the Confederates from General *Cleburne's* and General *Maney's* divisions. As you drive along Flat Shoals Road, *Cleburne* would have been attacking from your right and *Maney* from your left. Smith's Federal infantry crossed back and forth and fought from both sides of their trenches. One of the last Confederate assaults in this area occurred at 5 P.M. and forced G. A. Smith's division to withdraw northward to a position on the left of General Leggett's division entrenched on Bald Hill. During one of the heaviest of these attacks against Smith, Col. *Harris D. Lampley*, in command of the 45th Alabama Infantry of *Cleburne's* division, was taken prisoner by one of his Union counterparts, Col. William W. Belknap of the 15th Iowa Infantry. While leading his troops, Colonel *Lampley* was standing atop the Union trench when Colonel Belknap pulled *Lampley* into the earthwork and made the Southern leader a prisoner. Here as elsewhere, the fighting was so fierce that bayonets and swords often were the principal weapons. Gen. G. A. Smith's division incurred the heaviest losses of the Union troops engaged in the Battle of Atlanta. The division lost 1,041 men—approximately one-fourth of all the Federal casualties.

At the end of Flat Shoals Avenue turn right on Moreland Avenue. (The intersection is a tricky one; be sure to look for the one-way sign directing you to the left toward the intersection.) As you pass over I-20 notice that the ground rises slightly. This elevation was the site of Bald Hill, another important landmark of the Battle of Atlanta that was destroyed by the construction of the expressway. The hill was occupied by General Leggett's 17th Corps division and hence is sometimes known as Leggett's Hill. Leggett's men were entrenched facing to your left and

Looking south along Moreland Avenue toward its intersection with Interstate 20. The rise in the center of the photograph is what remains of Leggett's or Bald Hill, scene of some of the heaviest fighting during the Battle of Atlanta. The construction of I-20 eradicated all the crest of the hill. Federal Gen. Mortimer D. Leggett's 17th Corps division defended this eminence and was attacked from both the left and the right by several Confederate divisions, including those of Gens. *Patrick R. Cleburne* and *George Maney*. Late in the battle, Union forces fighting to the south around the present-day East Atlanta business district withdrew to Bald Hill and connected with Leggett's Federal division. The extension of this line, to the left (east) and beyond the view provided here, rendered the Union position impregnable and thus helped to secure a telling victory for Sherman's bluecoats.

Looking northeast toward Battery Place from the dirt mound at the northern end of the Inman Park-Reynoldstown MARTA station parking lot. Capt. Francis De Gress's Battery H, 1st Illinois Light Artillery, was located to the left of the white house pictured here. Extending to the right (southward) was Gen. Joseph A. J. Lightburn's 15th Corps brigade. These formations were among the Union forces attacked by two divisions of Confederate Gen. *Benjamin F. Cheatham's* corps. A portion of Gen. *John C. Brown's* Southern division assaulted the area encompassed by this photograph.

toward you. Like G. A. Smith's companion unit to the south, they were forced to fight from both sides of their trenches. When Smith's division withdrew to connect with Leggett's left toward the end of the day's fighting, other Union forces connected to Smith's left. These moves extended the Federal line eastward in the direction of Murphy High School. The joining of these units solidified the southern end of the Army of the Tennessee's position and thus rendered it impervious to further Confederate assaults. For the next half mile on Moreland Avenue, you will be driving north along the line of General Harrow's Union division, which also faced west and was assaulted from that direction by General *Clayton's* and General *Brown's* divisions of *Cheatham's* Confederate corps. A mile from I-20, Moreland passes under DeKalb Avenue and the Georgia Railroad. Just beyond the overpass, turn right onto the DeKalb Avenue exit. (Watch for a sign with an arrow pointing right.) The ramp will merge with DeKalb Avenue heading west back toward the center of Atlanta.

Drive .1 miles to the Inman Park-Reynoldstown MARTA station, and make a right turn into the parking lot. Drive to the far (north) end of the lot and park your car. Stand by the brown fence and face south toward the railroad station. To your right about two miles is the center of Atlanta; from that direction came the Southern forces that attacked the Union positions in this area. Upon the low ridge on your left is a line of wooden-frame houses. This rise was the location of a portion of the outer defensive line protecting Atlanta. General *Hood's* Confederates abandoned the line early on the morning of July 22. The move was intended to create a diversion that would occupy the attention of the Federals while *Hardee's* Confederate corps completed its flanking march and attacked the rear of McPherson's Army of the Tennessee.

Shortly before daylight, the Union forces discovered the empty Southern trenches in their front and moved forward to begin the process of reversing the works to accommodate the bluecoats. Throughout the day, the Federal units in this vicinity were busily engaged in their activities but no doubt heard the sound of the desperate fighting to the south. Between 3 and 4 P.M., as their work was proceeding, the Union forces here were assaulted by two full Confederate divisions.

Turn left and face the row of houses. At the time of the attack Gen. M. L. Smith's 15th Corps division was in the trenches on the small rise in front of you. That portion of the line was held by General Lightburn's brigade of M. L. Smith's division. Battery H, 1st Illinois Light Artillery, under the command of Capt. Francis De Gress, was posted at the left (north) end of the houses. To your right near the point where you entered the parking lot, two guns of Battery A, 1st Illinois Light Artillery, were located just north (this side) of the railroad close to a two-story house owned by the Widow Pope. South of the railroad and continuing the line of M. L. Smith's division was Colonel Martin's brigade, half of which had been sent earlier in the day to reinforce the left of General Sweeny's 16th Corps division. To the south of Martin was Harrow's 15th Corps division, the left of which joined the extreme right of General Blair's 17th Corps. Turn left and face north away from the train station. The high ground in the distance, which is obscured by trees in the warm months, was the location of the remaining division, commanded by General Woods of General Logan's 15th Corps.

Turn back around and face the station. The Confederate divisions that assaulted the Union positions here were in line-of-battle several hundred yards to your right. These divisions were commanded by General *Brown* and General *Clayton*, both from General *Cheatham's* corps. At the beginning of the day, these same troops had occupied the lines that Logan's Federals were reversing. In preparation for the attack,

Looking southeast toward Battery Place and the Inman Park-Reynoldstown MARTA station from the brown fence at the north end of the station's parking lot. In the center of the photograph stands a large hardwood tree that is the approximate location of the Widow Pope House. The commuter train station to the right stands roughly on the site of the Georgia Railroad cut that figured prominently in the late stages of the Battle of Atlanta. Gen. *Arthur M. Manigault's* Confederate brigade attacked successfully from right to left through and around the railroad cut. In the process a portion of Battery A, 1st Illinois Light Artillery, and the southward extension of General Lightburn's Federal brigade plus Capt. Francis De Gress's battery were overrun. Only the Union artillery pieces next to the railroad cut were removed from the battlefield by their Confederate captors. The area included in this and the previous photograph were the objects of the successful Union counterattack late in the afternoon of the battle. Also, the Grant Park Cyclorama of the Battle of Atlanta features the fighting that took place in the area of the MARTA station.

Brown's division was deployed astride the railroad with two of its brigades north of it and two south. The four brigades of *Clayton's* division were aligned on *Brown's* right.

As the Confederates approached this portion of the Union line, they were greeted by a storm of artillery and infantry fire. The initial Southern assault was rebuffed, and the troops sought shelter in a ravine about 400 yards to your right. There *Brown's* and *Clayton's* men rallied and renewed the attack. By this time, the area you are standing in was obscured by gunpowder smoke. When the Southerners tried the Union line again, they achieved unexpected success. Three infantry regiments, the 18th and 19th South Carolina and the 28th Alabama, from Gen. *Arthur M. Manigault's* brigade of *Brown's* division managed to pass undetected into the cut through which the Georgia Railroad ran. The cut was located about where the train station is situated. Once through, a number of men from the *19th South Carolina* ascended to the second story of the Widow Pope's house. From this elevation, the South Carolinians had a good shot at their Northern foes. The Union line here and to the south began to give way at about this time.

Lightburn's brigade and the remaining half of Martin's retreated eastward (to your left). The Illinois batteries in this area now had no infantry to protect them, so the cannoneers had to abandon their guns to the enemy. De Gress's artillerists, however, before they withdrew managed to render their guns useless by spiking them. *Manigault's* Confederate brigade, part of which advanced through the railroad cut, wheeled northward on the ridge topped by houses to your left. These troops captured the guns of De Gress's battery and attempted unsuccessfully to use the spiked cannon against the fleeing Northerners. To the south, beyond the train station, General Harrow's Union division was attacked in its front by *Clayton's* division and outflanked on its right by the Southerners who had broken through M. L. Smith's 15th Corps division. As a result, Harrow's two right brigades withdrew eastward.

The situation now appeared desperate for the Federals. The area you are in was completely overrun by Confederates. General Logan, who was about a mile east along the Georgia Railroad overseeing the placement of a division to cover that area against possible attack, was informed of developments in this area. Immediately he ordered the half of Martin's 15th Corps brigade that had reinforced the left of Sweeny's 16th Corps division to return to the endangered area. Logan also directed Colonel Mersy's brigade of Sweeny's division to withdraw from its position and move to reinforce the hard-pressed 15th Corps.

When Logan arrived at the Georgia Railroad, he, General Lightburn, and Gen. M. L. Smith organized a counterattack to retake the lost Union positions astride the tracks. The counterassault consisted of General Harrow's two brigades south of the railroad, all of M. L. Smith's division (the brigades of Lightburn and Martin) plus Mersy's 16th Corps brigade, and the two remaining brigades of General Woods's division to the north of the hole in the Federal lines. Six pieces of artillery were deployed along Woods's line to assist in the effort to throw *Brown's* and *Clayton's* Confederate divisions back.

Turn left and face the previously mentioned row of houses. The ground where you are standing was just about centered in the area that the Union forces attacked. In all, seven brigades from four divisions counterattacked the Southerners. The assault was a complete success. The lost territory was regained and the line of the 15th Corps restored. De Gress's artillerists were even able to retake their guns, unspike them, and turn them on the Confederates retreating westward through this area back toward Atlanta. Thus ended the battle of Atlanta, the largest and costliest engagement of the campaign.

This concludes the Battle of Atlanta tour. At this point you may choose to return toward Five Points to continue to the Ezra Church tour, or to take a recommended side trip to the Cyclorama. The Cyclorama is a spectacular 360-degree painting of the Battle of Atlanta which was prepared by a group of German and Polish artists in 1885-86. It is located in Grant Park and operated by the City of Atlanta. The presentation there includes an interpretive film and other exhibits.

Both options require that you leave the parking lot through the exit near the small row of businesses and get on Edgewood Avenue heading west. On your right soon after you enter Edgewood is Springvale Park. The park encompasses part of the ravine in which *Brown's* Confederate division took cover after its unsuccessful first charge into the line of the 15th Corps. About .7 miles from the park at Randolph Street you will be passing through the location of a portion of the inner circuit of defensive works that directly protected Atlanta.

To head toward Five Points, simply continue on Edgewood Avenue. To go directly to the Ezra Church tour or the Cyclorama, you will need to get on Interstate 75/85. To do this, go under the Interstate 75/85 overpass and make an immediate left onto the entrance ramp. Once up the ramp and into traffic, move over two lanes to the left. Follow the signs for Exit 92 East and West, being sure to avoid Exit 93 in the process. Exit 92 will take you to Interstate 20. After you go under the large, multi-lane overpass, you will bear left to go east to the Cyclorama or bear right to go west to the Ezra Church battlefield tour. Once on Interstate 20 East, go about .5 miles, take Exit 26 (Boulevard), and follow the signs to Grant Park, which will be on your right about a half mile south of the expressway. While at Grant Park and the Cyclorama you may wish to go to the southeast corner of the park to view one of the last remaining portions of the earthen fortifications that formed Atlanta's inner defensive circuit. To continue on to the Ezra Church tour, retrace your route along Boulevard and enter Interstate 20 West. (Turn left just across the expressway bridge onto Bryan Street; then turn left onto the interstate entrance ramp, being sure to carefully follow the I-20 West signs along the way.)

ATLANTA HISTORY

A Journal of Georgia and the South

■

ATLANTA HISTORY is published quarterly by the Atlanta Historical Society. Its 4,200 subscribers include members of the Society, libraries, schools and universities, and other historical societies throughout the country.

MANUSCRIPT CONTRIBUTORS are welcomed. Articles in *Atlanta History* focus not only on metropolitan Atlanta, but also on broader issues affecting Georgia and the South.

PLEASE SEND manuscript submissions or inquiries to the editor, Bradley R. Rice. Typescripts should be approximately fifteen to thirty-five pages long, not including end notes. All material must be double-spaced and placed at the end of the manuscript. The preferred style follows *The Chicago Manual of Style*, 13th edition. Manuscripts should be sent in duplicate to: Bradley R. Rice, Publications Department, Atlanta Historical Society, 3101 Andrews Drive, Atlanta, GA, 30305.

THE FRANKLIN GARRETT AWARD is given biannually for the best article dealing directly with Atlanta. The Alex Bealer Award, awarded on alternate years, recognizes the outstanding contributor on a non-Atlanta subject. Both awards convey a cash prize, certificate, and media recognition.

FACILITIES at the Atlanta Historical Society include a research library open to the public with ample study space and access to archival materials, which include many private collections as well as newspaper files; city directories; city, county and court records; and photograph files.

For further information contact Bradley R. Rice, editor, at (404) 961-3460 or the AHS publications manager at (404) 261-1837.

The Battle of Ezra Church:
Tour Three

General Description of the Battle

After the Battle of Atlanta, Sherman decided to approach the city from a different direction in his ceaseless efforts to cut *Hood's* avenues of supply, the railroads leading into Atlanta. Convinced that the Confederate government in Richmond was now aware of the imminent threat posed to Atlanta and would soon send heavy reinforcements to aid in its defense, Sherman resolved to press hard against Atlanta's defenders in an attempt to bring them to decisive battle. Through the engagement on July 22, the Union forces had been extending their lines around Atlanta from the north to the east. With the Battle of Atlanta won and the severed Georgia Railroad in Union hands (as well as the Western and Atlantic which was the Federal supply route), Sherman determined on a southward advance along the west side of Atlanta to threaten East Point, the juncture of the Macon and Western (M&W, now the Central of Georgia) and the Atlanta and West Point (A&WP) Railroads. These two railroads were *Hood's* last avenues of supply. The M&W connected Atlanta to Macon and Savannah. The A&WP joined the city to Alabama and Mississippi.

To accomplish this mission, Sherman chose the Army of the Tennessee, fresh from victory on July 22. In conjunction with the move by the infantry to capture East Point, Sherman accepted a plan by his cavalry commanders to launch a mounted raid aimed at destroying the M&W tracks in the vicinity of Lovejoy's Station, about twenty-two miles south of Atlanta. The idea behind this maneuver was to break *Hood's* most vital remaining rail line and to create a diversion to aid the infantry in their march to East Point. If they accomplished their goal at Lovejoy's, the Union horsemen had Sherman's permission to continue southward to free the thousands of Federal soldiers imprisoned at Macon and at Camp Sumter, better known as Andersonville.

The operation began on the evening of July 26, when the Army of the Tennessee was withdrawn from its positions on the east side of Atlanta. To mask the movement, a contingent of Union cavalry occupied the vacated Federal trenches astride the Georgia Railroad, and the Armies of the Cumberland and the Ohio sent detachments of infantry to engage *Hood's* Confederates in the fortifications before Atlanta.

Despite the diversionary tactics, as early as July 27 *Hood* was aware of the Federal moves. He notified the Confederate garrisons at Macon and Andersonville of the possibility of Union cavalry coming their way, and he dispatched a portion of his own cavalry to intercept the raiders. To counter the move by Sherman's infantry to sever his remaining railroads, *Hood* conceived an intricate plan similar in form to *Hardee's* flanking maneuver that resulted in the Battle of Atlanta. Gen. *Stephen D. Lee's* corps was ordered to advance westward from the city to engage the Army of the Tennessee and thus freeze its movement. At the same time, Gen. *Alexander P. Stewart's* troops were to maneuver around the exposed right flank of the Federals and destroy them.

Sherman elevated Gen. Oliver O. Howard, who had been directing the 4th Corps of the Army of the Cumberland, to the command of the Army of the Tennessee on July 27. The death of McPherson on the twenty-second had placed Sherman in a quandary. He had to find an officer of talent and one who could be trusted to obey orders promptly. After conferring with General Thomas, his most trusted subordinate, Sherman decided upon Howard, a fellow West Pointer who appeared to be the best man available for the job. Sherman immediately ordered Howard to put his troops in motion, and by 10 A.M. on the morning of July 28, Howard's army was moving into place on the west side of Atlanta.

The line taken up by Howard's Federals was much like a square root symbol. (Map 9) On its north end it connected with a portion of Thomas's Army of the Cumberland. Gen. Grenville A. Dodge's 16th Corps was on the left, running roughly north to south and facing east toward Atlanta. The line of this corps was astride Simpson Street, extending more or less along the course of Chappell Road with its right curving sharply to the west toward West Lake Avenue. Gen. Frank P. Blair's 17th Corps joined the center of Dodge's line at Simpson Street and continued southward on the same high ridge to a point somewhat north of Ezra Church, the Methodist meeting house that gave this battle its name and that stood at the southeast corner of Mozley Park. Gen. John A. Logan's 15th Corps, beginning with Gen. Charles R. Woods's division, extended the line to a low rise south of Martin Luther King, Jr., Drive near the intersection of Laurel Avenue and Archer Street. On this eminence the position formed an exposed, salient angle as it turned northwestward. Gen. William Harrow's division occupied this sector and was joined on its right by Gen. Morgan L. Smith's division. The right flank of the latter was refused or curved back northward to protect it from possible flanking maneuvers by the Confederates. The line of Harrow and M. L. Smith extended along a natural ridge that stretches northwestward from the salient and cuts across Martin Luther King, Jr., Drive and West Lake Avenue. The ridge ends in the vicinity of a high hill partly taken up by Anderson Park. Thus deployed, Howard's troops were in position to fulfill Sherman's purpose, that is, to extend the Union line toward East Point and thereby force *Hood* to confront their lines and overextend himself to the point that he would have to give up Atlanta.

The first Confederate corps to arrive on the scene and deploy was that of Gen. *Stephen D. Lee* (not related to Gen. *Robert E. Lee*). Gen. *John C. Brown's* division was put in line-of-battle near the northern boundary of Westview Cemetery, facing the Union division of M. L. Smith. *Lee's* remaining division, that of Gen. *Henry D. Clayton*, was aligned along a portion of Westview Drive eastward from its intersection with Gordon Street. This Confederate division also faced northward but directly at the strongly defended Federal salient formed by Harrow's and Woods's divisions.

During the forenoon of July 28, the Army of the Tennessee was busily erecting barricades, a form of light field entrenchments, to protect its position. This activity was done with especial vigor by the soldiers of the 15th Corps, who would bear the brunt of the impending battle, because their position formed the extreme right of Sherman's armies and was thus exposed. The troops of Col. Hugo Wangelin's brigade of Woods's 15th Corps division even resorted to removing the benches from Ezra Church and then buttressing these with their knapsacks to serve as cover.

At approximately noon, *Brown's* Confederate division, forming the left of *Lee's* corps, began the battle by storming M. L. Smith's Federal line. The repeated attacks by this Southern unit reached the Union breastworks and even managed to turn M. L. Smith's right flank. Gen. Charles C. Walcutt's brigade of Harrow's division, then being held in reserve behind the main Federal line, was called on to supply two regiments to buttress Smith's endangered flank. These regiments, as well as several others from the 16th and 17th Corps (not engaged in the battle), were able not only to check the flanking move of *Brown's* Confederates but also to outflank them. Once this brief crisis had been resolved, M. L. Smith's Federals held firm through several more hours of assaults.

General *Clayton's* Southern division, *Brown's* companion unit on the right, moved forward around 1 P.M. to attack the Union salient in the vicinity of Ezra Church. This assault fell largely on the left brigade of Harrow's 15th Corps division and the right brigade of General Woods's division of the same corps. On this portion of the battlefield, the woods came within fifty yards of the salient angle. Thus the Confederates emerged from the timber nearly on top of the Union line. Only two of *Clayton's* brigades actually participated in the attack, the third being withheld. The lead brigade, that of Gen. *Randall L. Gibson*, moved forward under orders from a corps staff officer and struck the well-fortified Federal salient without support. This command error occurred while General *Gibson* was in the rear of the division and therefore unable to direct his troops in person. *Gibson's* Confederates drove within a few yards of the Federal line, which was reinforced at the very point of the salient by the remaining three regiments from General Walcutt's 15th Corps reserve brigade. When General *Clayton* learned that his lead brigade was being stopped short of the Union line, he ordered another of his brigades, Gen. *Alpheus Baker's*, to assist *Gibson*. Despite the effort of these two units, the Federal position about Ezra Church could not be overrun. Toward the end of the battle, *Clayton's* Southerners withdrew from the field under the protective fire of the remaining brigade of the division.

In the midst of General *S. D. Lee's* attempts to break the Union line, General *Stewart's* corps arrived. It had been charged with the task of delivering the *coup de grace* to Howard's Army of the Tennessee by marching around the Union right flank and attacking its rear. At *Lee's* suggestion, *Stewart's* lead division, Gen. *Edward C. Walthall's*, was placed in line-of-battle in rear of *Brown's* division. This deployment constituted disobedience of General *Hood's* orders, but the attempts so far to breach Logan's 15th Corps line were unsuccessful and needed reinforcement. By about 2 P.M., *Brown's* Confederate division had retired from the field. Beginning around 3 P.M. and continuing for two hours, *Walthall's* Southerners repeatedly assaulted the high ground occupied by M. L. Smith's Union division, the same unit attacked earlier in the battle by *Brown's* troops. On the right of the Confederate position, General *Clayton* renewed his attempts to break the Federal line, but the result was the same as for all of *Hood's* troops on that day: many killed and wounded with no success.

At this point in the battle, General *Stewart* was on a small rise near the Federal salient surveying the situation. Shortly before, *Stewart's* remaining division on the scene, Gen. *William W. Loring's*, had been aligned for battle in support of *Clayton's* division. Before he could order *Loring* into battle, *Stewart* was struck by a spent ball, a bullet that had ricocheted off some object, and he was carried wounded from the field. The command of *Stewart's* corps fell to his senior division commander present, *General Walthall*. Seeing that any effort to continue the battle would be wasteful of men and futile in the extreme, *Walthall* withdrew *Stewart's* corps, and *S. D. Lee* did likewise with his corps. The withdrawal took place around 5 P.M., and by 10 P.M. the battle-weary Confederates were on Lick Skillet Road, now known as Gordon Street, heading back into Atlanta's protective fortifications.

As Logan's 15th Corps was approaching and then fortifying the Ezra Church area, Sherman was some two miles away in the company of a group of officers. One of the officers was Major James A. Connolly, who recorded Sherman's observations in a letter home. As the sounds of musketry and artillery grew to the din of battle, Sherman declared: "Logan is feeling for them and I guess he has found them." In a short while a staff officer from General Howard sped up on his horse and related the course of the battle to that point. Revealing his pleasure at *Hood's* decision to attack yet again, Sherman exclaimed: "Good! That's fine! Just what I wanted, just what I wanted! Tell Howard to invite them to attack. It will save us trouble, save us trouble. They'll only beat their own brains out, beat their own brains out." Straightway, Sherman ordered his other two armies to press hard upon the fortifications of Atlanta in an attempt to find a weak point caused by the departure from the city of the Confederate troops that were attacking Howard around Ezra Church. The Armies of the Cumberland and the Ohio tried Atlanta's defenses but found them to be strong and well-manned. No further effort was made that day to test the city's defensive works. In the final movement of the battle, twenty-six pieces of artillery from the Army of the Tennessee were moved to an area north of Logan's extreme right flank. The guns were intended to protect that flank against any further efforts to break the Union position in the Ezra Church area.

Like his two earlier attempts at Peachtree Creek and the Battle of Atlanta, this sally forth from fortifications to attack Sherman's Federals and halt their encircling moves had cost *Hood* dearly. Of the 18,450 engaged, Confederate casualties numbered approximately 4,300. The Union losses, on the other hand, totaled only 632 out of 13,226 that participated. Admittedly, *Hood* halted (though only temporarily) Sherman's extension toward East Point, but once again direct assaults by Confederate troops on Federals defending from behind field entrenchments had resulted in disaster. Also, the Southern divisions attacked in piecemeal, uncoordinated fashion, just as they had done during the Battle of Atlanta. This failure in generalship could possibly have been corrected by *Hood's* being on the scene to direct the battle in person. The only tangible result of the several Confederate attacks on July 28 was the slaughter of thousands of men who were badly needed for the protection of Atlanta. The Battle of Ezra Church had almost thoroughly broken the fighting spirit of *Hood's* Army of Tennessee. The old determination of this veteran army, noticeably evident during General *Johnston's* tenure as its commander, was now gone. Its disappearance would play a pivotal role in the remaining efforts to hold Atlanta against its Union assailants. In just eleven days of army command, *Hood's* losses totaled 14,800. By contrast, *J. E. Johnston's* losses from the beginning of the campaign up to the time he was relieved on July 17 were approximately 11,600. *Hood* had done more damage through casualties in eleven days than *Johnston* had done in ten weeks. In short, *Hood* was in the process of bleeding his army white in vain efforts to maintain possession of the railroads, his lines of supply and communication.

For the Confederates, the news from south of Atlanta was better. The Union cavalry raid, for which Sherman had high hopes, had ended in failure. Because of a lack of coordination, the effort by the cavalry resulted in only a temporary break of the M&W Railroad, and a large portion of the troopers who were attempting to free their comrades at Macon and Andersonville later surrendered. By August 4, the remnants of Sherman's horsemen had limped back to Marietta, there to reorganize. Sherman had never had a great deal of faith in the ability or usefulness of cavalry, and this episode only further convinced him of his belief.

Following the Ezra Church encounter, Sherman withdrew portions of Thomas's Army of the Cumberland and all of Schofield's Army of the Ohio from their trenches about Atlanta to extend Howard's right toward East Point. Federals and Confederates alike now settled into a period known as the Siege of Atlanta that lasted from July 28 to August 25. This stage was punctuated with cavalry raids by both sides and ended at Jonesboro in Sherman's last and successful attempt to destroy the remaining railroads provisioning Atlanta.

Looking north along Chappell Road toward its intersection with Bankhead Highway, which runs left to right. In the distance on the hill are the Overlook Atlanta apartments. Gen. Jefferson C. Davis's 14th Corps division (temporarily commanded by Gen. James D. Morgan) occupied the hill. Davis's division was sent to reinforce Gen. Oliver O. Howard's Army of the Tennessee (south of this point) but was unable to complete the maneuver.

The Driving Tour of the Ezra Church Battlefield
(approximately 7.7 miles)

Proceed west on I-20 about **1.5** miles from the I-75/85 interchange near the Atlanta-Fulton County Stadium. (Map 10) Get off I-20 at Exit 19 and turn right (north) onto Ashby Street. About **.5** miles from the expressway, Ashby intersects Fair Street. The northeast corner of this intersection is occupied by Moravian Baptist Church and was the location of the earthen fort that was the farthest westward extension of the inner circuit of Confederate defenses protecting Atlanta. From this point, the inner fortifications ran gradually northeastward and southeastward back toward Atlanta. After the Battle of Ezra Church on July 28, *Hood's* forces erected a line of fortifications that began at Fair Street and ran southwestward (diagonally away from Moravian Church) to East Point. The purpose of this line of works was to protect the last open railroads that met at East Point and ran from there into Atlanta as a single track.

Continue on Ashby Street for another **1.6** miles to Bankhead Highway and turn left (west). (The intersection is at the top of a fairly steep rise, and there is a left-turn-only lane.) One mile from Ashby, turn left (south) onto Chappell Road. On the right just before the turn is a prominent height known as Davis Hill, which is the location of the Overlook Atlanta apartments. In late July 1864, this hill was occupied by the Federal troops of Gen. Jefferson C. Davis's division of the 14th Corps. The night before the fight at Ezra Church, Sherman had ordered Davis's troops (temporarily under the command of Gen. James D. Morgan because of Davis's ill health) to reinforce the right of Howard's army. Sherman was anxious to have his forces placed so that a Confederate flanking maneuver similar to the one on July 22 could not be repeated. Because it lacked guides and decent maps, the column got lost and was ordered by Sherman back to its original position. Sherman himself later speculated that if Morgan had been in place by the time of the Confederate assaults at Ezra Church, he could not only have defeated the Southerners but could have thoroughly routed them.

Chappell Road roughly parallels the July 28 positions of the Union forces of the 16th, 17th, and a portion of the 15th Corps. (About **.5** miles south of the intersection of Chappell and Bankhead Highway, be sure to stay on Chappell by bearing right at the "Y" intersection with Mayson Turner Road.) Drive another **.5** miles to Ezra Church Drive. This road will be on your right before Chappell crosses over a set of

Looking northeast toward Sadie G. Mays Memorial Nursing Home, the site of the previous Battle Hill Sanitarium for the treatment of tuberculosis. Waterbury Drive runs from left to right. Gen. Joseph A. J. Lightburn's brigade of Gen. Morgan L. Smith's 15th Corps division defended the ground now occupied by the retirement home and faced Waterbury. The Battle of Ezra Church began in this area as Gen. *John C. Brown's* Confederate division assaulted M. L. Smith's Federals at approximately noon on July 28, 1864. After *Brown* was repulsed, Gen. *Edward C. Walthall's* Southern division attempted to storm Smith's Union line but was also rebuffed.

railroad tracks. Turn right onto Ezra Church Drive. The road will ascend to a height that forms part of the ridge along which the bulk of Howard's army faced east (behind you) toward Atlanta. Continue on Ezra Church for .7 miles till it runs into West Lake Avenue. Turn left, travel .3 miles, and turn right on Calloway Drive.

As you drive along Calloway, you are approaching the area where the Battle of Ezra Church began. Drive .3 miles, and Calloway will intersect Anderson Avenue. Turn left onto Anderson and come to a stop on the side of the road. You are on high ground that is the continuation of the ridge system occupied by General Logan's 15th Corps on July 28. The high ground in this immediate area was occupied by Gen. M. L. Smith's division which formed the extreme right flank of the Union forces operating against Atlanta. Farther to your right (west), beyond the hill, there were no Union forces when the battle began. It was this exposed flank that the Confederates were attempting to turn. The battle began in this vicinity as General *Brown's* division of *Lee's* Confederate corps attacked the Federal positions around you. *Brown's* Southerners would have been coming straight at you, and they managed to lap around M. L. Smith's right, which was on the high ground to your right. Two regiments from General Walcutt's 15th Corps reserve brigade, plus about a dozen regiments from the 16th and 17th Corps, were rushed to this endangered area. The Union forces already here had been forced to withdraw slightly, but with the help of the reinforcements, they were able to restore the original line and outflank their Confederate assailants.

Continue on to the stop sign where Anderson temporarily ends. Make a left onto Waterbury Drive. Travel .1 miles to the end of Waterbury and turn right onto the continuation of Anderson. As you drive along Waterbury, *Brown's* Confederates would have been advancing from your right to your left in their repeated assaults on M. L. Smith's Federals. After *Brown* failed to break the Union position to your left, his division was withdrawn. It was replaced by *Walthall's* division of General *Stewart's* Confederate corps. Beginning around 3 P.M. on that afternoon, *Walthall* tried unsuccessfully for two hours to break the same Union position that *Brown* had stormed.

Proceed .3 miles on Anderson, and be sure to stay in the right lane when it widens into two lanes. (You are coming to a tricky intersection,

Looking south along Laurel Avenue toward Interstate 20, from the site of the Federal salient angle occupied just after the battle began by three Union regiments from Gen. Charles C. Walcutt's reserve brigade, 15th Corps. The slight rise in the distance is what remains of the ridge that sheltered Gen. *Henry D. Clayton's* division while it prepared to charge the Union salient. Most of the ridge was destroyed by I-20 construction.

so follow the directions carefully.) Anderson ends at its intersection with Martin Luther King, Jr., Drive. At the traffic light turn left, and stay on the road that runs along the cemetery fence. You are now on Gordon Street, and Westview Cemetery is on your right. *Walthall's* and *Brown's* Confederate divisions aligned for battle in that portion of the cemetery nearest Gordon.* The cemetery gate is on the right about .3

---

* The cemetery, established in 1884, contains a Confederate memorial statue, about which are buried Southern soldiers who survived the war. Information concerning the location of the memorial can be obtained at the cemetery office.

miles from where you turned onto Gordon Street. On the left as you enter the gate is the cemetery office. Directly across from the gate is Westview Drive. Turn left onto Westview and drive slowly as you pass over I-20 on a bridge. General *Clayton's* division of General *S. D. Lee's* Confederate corps deployed in line-of-battle in this area.

After the bridge, take the first left, which is Matthewson Place. Drive .2 miles to Mims Street and turn left. Proceed two blocks and turn right where Mims ends at Laurel Avenue. Drive .1 miles to Archer Street which will join Laurel from the right. Stop here and face the direction from which you have just traveled. You are now looking south. The intersection of Laurel and Archer was the location of the southern point of the Federal salient angle during the Battle of Ezra Church. This immediate area was heavily wooded. As you face south, notice that Laurel descends to a low point and then starts to rise again. The construction of I-20 took the rest of the ridge that you can see beginning to ascend. Beyond what used to be the ridge lies another low area. There *Clayton's* Confederates were able to deploy for battle, sheltered by the ridge from the watchful eyes of the Federals. The path that *Clayton's* division took to the Union works at Laurel and Archer brought them straight at you. The attack in this area of the battlefield began around 1 P.M. Turn around and face north along the continuation of Laurel.

You are facing the Union salient. When the battle began, this portion

Looking north toward the intersection of Laurel Avenue and Archer Street. The first house on the right stands on the site of the apex of the Federal salient. *Clayton's* **Confederates were sheltered by woods south of this point before reaching a fifty-yard clearing in front of the salient.**

Looking northwest toward the southeast corner of Mozley Park. Martin Luther King, Jr. Drive is on the left. Ezra Church stood on the rise to the right. A portion of the Union line ran from left to right and faced the road in the foreground. This area was defended by Col. Hugo Wangelin's 15th Corps brigade, which used soldiers' knapsacks and the church's wooden pews for breastworks.

of the Federal line was partly occupied by Col. John M. Oliver's brigade of General Harrow's 15th Corps division. From this point northeastward (to your right) for a distance of 100 yards there were no Union troops. Because of the thick woods, *Clayton's* Confederates were able to approach within fifty yards of Oliver's Federals before being seen. The initial Southern assaults here posed a great threat to the Union line because of the hundred-yard gap. This menace was countered by moving three infantry regiments from General Walcutt's 15th corps reserve brigade into the vacant interval. The regiments were the 103rd Illinois, the 97th Indiana, and the 46th Ohio. Here as elsewhere along the Union line, the numerous Confederate assaults were unable to defeat the Federals who fought behind hastily built but sturdy field entrenchments.

Get back in your car and continue northward on Laurel till it ends at Martin Luther King, Jr., Drive. Turn right and drive .2 miles to Mozley Park. Turn left into the parking lot. Stand on the high grassy area and face Martin Luther King, Jr., Drive. The Methodist meeting house known as Ezra Church, which gave this battle its name, stood on this ground. The troops of Col. Hugo Wangelin's brigade of General Woods's 15th Corps division removed benches from the church to help fortify their position. A portion of *Clayton's* Confederate division repeatedly attacked this position during the Ezra Church battle. Only the right of Wangelin's brigade, which fought in this immediate area and faced to your left, was engaged. The Federal position here was not broken, and about 5 P.M. the Confederates gave up their futile attempts to breach their foe's line. Thus ended the Battle of Ezra Church. To leave, turn right out of the parking lot and go back along Martin Luther King, Jr., Drive .5 miles to I-20 East. (The intersection is complicated.) Following the I-20 East sign, turn left under the bridge to enter the expressway back toward downtown. To continue on to the next tour, take Exit 23 and travel south on I-75 toward Macon.

As you drive along Martin Luther King, Jr., Drive toward I-20, you will pass the high ground on your left where Confederate General *Stewart* was wounded while leading his corps. He was taken from the field but returned to duty about two-and-one-half weeks later. At the time he was shot, *Stewart* was about to send his remaining division into battle. His senior division commander, General *Walthall,* removed *Stewart's* corps, which was followed by *Lee's* corps, from the field. No further attempts were made to break the Union line, and around 10 p.m. the Confederates who survived the fight at Ezra Church withdrew into Atlanta's defensive perimeter.

The Battle of Jonesboro:
Tour Four
General Description of the Battle

As the siege of Atlanta dragged on into the third week of August 1864, Sherman decided to give his cavalry one more chance to isolate *Hood's* army by cutting the M&W Railroad. On August 18, Gen. Judson Kilpatrick set out with a force of Federal cavalry to a point south of Jonesboro, a small town on the M&W Railroad sixteen miles south of Atlanta. There the Union horsemen attempted to wreck the tracks but were forced to withdraw by Gen. *William H. Jackson's* Confederate cavalrymen and a group of Southern infantry. The day after the attack, with the damage to the railroad repaired, supplies came into Atlanta as usual.

This latest experience with cavalry convinced Sherman that only infantry could successfully demolish a railroad. On August 25, therefore, Sherman withdrew his armies from the siege lines about Atlanta. He sent Gen. Henry W. Slocum's 20th Corps to protect the W&A Railroad bridge and other crossings over the Chattahoochee River. Sherman ordered the balance of his armies, six corps and attached formations, to begin marching to the vicinity of Sandtown near the Chattahoochee River and Red Oak Station, a small village on the A&WP Railroad about eleven miles from the center of Atlanta. This railroad joined the M&W at East Point, from whence they ran as a single track into Atlanta. (Map 11) Before the Union move got underway, *Hood* sent Gen. *Joseph Wheeler's* Confederate cavalry corps on a raid behind Union lines to cut the W&A Railroad, which was Sherman's supply line north to Chattanooga, Tennessee, and beyond. *Wheeler's* raid enjoyed only limited success against the W&A, and any further expectations for it were dashed when *Wheeler* veered into east Tennessee and away from Sherman's railroad supply lines running through the central portion of that state. With the departure of the bulk of his cavalry, *Hood* was deprived of precise knowledge of Sherman's moves late in August, but the Confederate commander was at least aware of the general direction of the Federal marches.

Sherman had assigned lines of march to each of his three army commanders. Through the first few days of operations, Federal columns closed in on their principal objective—Jonesboro. Schofield led his army to the village of Rough and Ready (recently called Mountain View), which was on the M&W a few miles north of Jonesboro. Thomas's Army of the Cumberland passed through Red Oak Station, tore up the tracks there, and then continued on to the M&W at a point midway between Rough and Ready and Jonesboro. Howard's troops, the victors at the Battles of Atlanta and Ezra Church, marched eastward through Fairburn in the direction of Jonesboro, where they were expected to wreck the M&W and thereby sever *Hood's* remaining supply line once and for all. (Map 12)

Hood's response to the Federal moves was to send portions of his army to intercept the Union forces as they neared the M&W. For the operation, *Hardee* was put in command of a force consisting of his own corps, temporarily under Gen. *Patrick R. Cleburne,* and Gen. *Stephen D. Lee's* corps. *Cleburne's* troops were sent to Rough and Ready, while *Lee's* men were directed to occupy East Point. A small detachment of infantry and cavalry was sent to Jonesboro to warn of any Union threats in that area. Thus, a line of Confederate formations stretching along the M&W from East Point to Jonesboro would be in a position to defend that vital supply route. (Map 13)

General Howard's Union Army of the Tennessee advanced toward Jonesboro principally by way of Fairburn Road, which crossed the Flint River about a mile and a half west of Jonesboro. (This is roughly the path of Georgia Highway 138 today). Here, the Union cavalrymen drove their Confederate counterparts away from the bridge. Howard's men then began to cross over to the high ground east of the river, which at this point was not much more than a swampy creek. The rest of the Union armies converging on Jonesboro spent the day destroying railroad tracks in the usual Federal way by heating the rails and bending them into loops that were known as "Sherman's Neckties." Theodore F. Upson, a Yankee private from Indiana, described this process which made it impossible to repair the railroad with the old rails:

> The way this was done is to string troops out along the track, two men to a tie. The men stick their guns with their bayonets on into the ground close behind them so as to have them handy in case of an attack, and then at a 'Yo heave!!' every man grabs a tie and lifts. Up comes the track and slowly tips over. Then with sledge hammers, hand spikes, or anything else handy, the ties are knocked loose from the rails, the fish plates unbolted, the pine ties made into piles, set on fire, and the rails laid on top. When they get red hot in the center about 20 men get hold of the ends and wind them edgewise around a telegraph pole or small tree. That fixes them.

A pile of crossties ready to be set afire and the rails atop bent into "Sherman's Neckties." (LC)

Sherman's Federals hard at work separating rails from times. This view was taken during the destruction of Atlanta's war resources prior to Sherman's March to the Sea in late 1864. The ruins of the W&A car shed are visible on the right beyond the soldiers. (LC)

The Battle of Jonesboro: First Day

By late afternoon of August 31, General Howard's three corps were deployed on both the east and west banks of the Flint River. (Map 14) On the east side of the river, the position was composed of a ridge line about three-quarters of a mile west of the M&W which ran north and south through Jonesboro. Through the ridge system ran Fairburn Road, which extended east to Jonesboro and west across the Flint to and beyond the Renfroe Plantation. Converging on the Renfroe place the day before, Howard's men moved westward on Fairburn Road toward the Flint River in order to replenish their canteens after a fatiguing march southward from the trenches about Atlanta. Logan's 15th Corps formed the center of Howard's position and lay astride Fairburn Road. On the right of Logan and extending westward across the river was Gen. Thomas E. G. Ransom's 16th Corps. Running northwestward on the west bank of the Flint River was Gen. Frank P. Blair's 17th Corps. Before and during the first day's fighting, one of Blair's divisions was moved to the east bank and deployed on Logan's left to provide support for that flank of the 15th Corps. Early next morning, the remaining division of the 17th Corps took a position on the left of the division that had already arrived and thus extended Blair's line toward the Flint River. By the time of the Confederate attack upon the Union forces in mid-afternoon of August 31, the units of Howard's Federals had become somewhat intermingled, but the geographic position of the army remained the same.

Beginning during the night of August 30-31, *Hood* sent *Hardee's* and *Lee's* corps to parry Sherman's thrust toward Jonesboro. Once the movement was underway, *Hood* summoned these two generals to Atlanta for a conference. The resulting plan called for *Hardee*, with the two corps under his command, to attack Howard and drive the Army of the Tennessee back west across the Flint River. *Lee's* corps would then be sent back toward Atlanta to attack the left of Sherman's forces that were operating against the railroads. The result, *Hood* hoped, would be to drive all the Union forces threatening Jonesboro back to the Chattahoochee River. All of *Lee's* and *Cleburne's* corps had not yet arrived at Jonesboro by the morning of August 31, the time *Hood* had set for the attack. Not until approximately 1:30 P.M. were the last of the weary Confederates in place and ready for battle. *Cleburne's* three divisions, commanded by Gens. *Mark P. Lowrey, John C. Brown,* and *George E. Maney,* were deployed in the vicinity of the intersection of Fayetteville Road (Georgia Highway 54) and Flint River Road, facing northwestward in the direction of a deep gully that protected a portion of the Union line and that would be an important factor in the first day's fighting at Jonesboro. *Lee's* corps, composed of the divisions of Gens. *Patton Anderson, Henry D. Clayton,* and *Carter L. Stevenson,* was positioned along Fayetteville Road in the vicinity of its intersection with North Avenue (Georgia Highway 138), facing west toward the Federal position.

Hardee planned to begin the attack by advancing *Cleburne's* corps, which would strike the right of the Union line. The sound of *Cleburne's* artillery, indicating a general engagement, would be *Lee's* signal to join the battle. If everything went as planned, *Hardee* would drive Howard's Federals westward across the Flint River and northward away from the M&W.

Howard expected that his position would be attacked, so he put his troops to work erecting barricades and digging trenches during the time prior to the Confederate assaults. The Confederate delay would prove to be costly, for Howard had anticipated that the attack would come early in the morning when he was more vulnerable. Howard expressed his concern when he wrote in his official report: "I had really expected an attack all day on account of the saucy position we occupied, since our artillery and even musketry reached the enemy's principal line of communication [the M&W Railroad]."

Around 3 P.M., hours late, *Cleburne's* corps at last advanced, and his skirmishers clashed with Federal pickets. The noise from this fight deceived *S. D. Lee* into believing that the battle itself had begun, so he prematurely advanced his corps and struck Howard's army, principally the front of Logan's 15th Corps. The Federals fired from behind hastily built field entrenchments and quickly repulsed *Lee's* corps. To the south, *Cleburne's* divisions advanced into the gully protecting Howard's right, and their lines became broken. This Confederate attack also fell on a body of Federal cavalry under General Kilpatrick, which was chased across the Flint River. *Hardee* sent word to *Lee* requesting that *Lee* renew his assault. *Lee* replied that this was impossible because of the timidity of his troops during their first attempt on the Union line. Consequently, *Hardee* ordered all the Confederates to break off their attacks and withdraw. Thus the first day's fighting at Jonesboro came to an end. The Confederate losses were staggering when compared to those of the Federals. Out of 23,811 engaged, *Hardee's* forces suffered 1,725 casualties. By contrast, the Union losses were only 179 out of 14,170. Once again, poorly coordinated Confederate attacks against entrenched Union positions resulted in an enormous disparity of casualties and a Confederate defeat with dire consequences.

Even before he knew the results of the fighting at Jonesboro, *Hood* had apparently decided that Atlanta would have to be given up. Ordered to East Point late in the evening of August 31, *Lee's* corps helped cover the evacuation of the city. (Map 15) At Jonesboro, *Hardee* had to overextend his line in order to cover the front of his and *Lee's* corps. Though he was ordered to prevent further destruction of the M&W and to protect Macon from a possible Federal thrust in that direction, *Hardee's* position at Jonesboro actually assisted in shielding the Confederate withdrawal from Atlanta. From the available evidence, it is impossible to know just exactly what was going on in *Hood's* mind concerning Atlanta's abandonment or perhaps its last-ditch defense. *Hood's* removal of his army's subsistence and a large portion of its ordnance stores to Jonesboro for safety before the Battle of Jonesboro and his removal of *Lee's* corps to the East Point area, however, argue for the interpretation that he had already determined to give over possession of the city to the Federals.

The Battle of Jonesboro: Second Day

Sherman on August 31 ordered Thomas and Schofield to advance their armies to the M&W at a point north of Jonesboro. (Map 16) From there, they would proceed south along the tracks and attempt to seize the town. Gen. Jefferson C. Davis's 14th Corps arrived first, and around 5 P.M. on September 1, it assaulted the northern portion of the Confederate line in the vicinity of the Warren House, north of the Confederate Cemetery in Jonesboro. At the same time, Howard's troops engaged *Hardee's* front west of the town in order to prevent any reinforcements from being sent to counter the attack of the 14th Corps. Davis's assault successfully breached the Southern position; a large portion of Gen. *Daniel C. Govan's* Confederate brigade was captured along with its commander, and two Rebel artillery batteries were also taken. Gen. David S. Stanley's 4th Corps was summoned by Sherman to move forward and assist Davis in possibly capturing all of *Hardee's* Confederate corps. Davis, however, was delayed by rough terrain and did not arrive until darkness had set in—too late to assist in the assault. In an attempt to prevent any Confederates from retreating southward, Sherman sent word for Blair to position his 17th Corps astride the M&W south of Jonesboro at Lovejoy's Station. The cavalry officer detailed to guide Blair's troops took too long a route, and the move was not completed. Sherman's final maneuver of the day was to order Gen. Henry W. Slocum to advance his corps toward Atlanta and test the strength of the Confederates remaining there.

Statistics for the Southern casualties on the second day of fighting at Jonesboro are incomplete, but *Hardee* lost well over 1,000 of a total of 12,661. Because of the frontal assault of the 14th Corps, the Federals suffered 1,169 casualties of 20,460 engaged. Over the course of the two-day battle at Jonesboro, *Hood's* forces incurred about twice as many casualties as Sherman's—roughly 2,700 Southerners to approximately 1,300 Northerners. Again the Confederates were paying a high price in lives without achieving commensurate results.

For the fourth time since his promotion to commander of the Confederate Army of Tennessee, *Hood* had sallied forth from the protection of Atlanta's trenches to attack Federal forces that were defending behind temporary but strong barricades made of wooden

Looking east along the Georgia Railroad in the direction of Decatur, with the remains of *Hood's* ordnance train and the ruins of the Confederate naval rolling mill in the center of the photograph. Today the Fulton Bag and Cotton Mill occupies the site of the 1864 rolling mill. See Battle of Atlanta Driving Tour, page 53. (LC)

rails and logs covered in front with earth. And once again the Confederates lost, even though on the second day Union General Davis's 14th Corps itself had engaged in costly frontal assault. *Hood* erred in not being present at Jonesboro to lead his troops in person. Instead, he turned over command of the Southern forces there to his old nemesis, General *Hardee*. This time, *Hood's* defeat had far-reaching effects. He gave up Atlanta and thereby passed control of the Gate City of the South and the Confederacy's most important railroad junction to the Federals. With Georgia cut nearly in half, Sherman was in position to proceed southward, slash the eastern Confederacy in two, and thus bring the tenets of the Anaconda Plan and the destruction of the Southern secessionist cause nearly to fulfillment.

On the evening of September 1, *Hood's* three corps were spread out from Atlanta to Jonesboro to cover the city's evacuation. (Map 17) Throughout the night, a series of thunderous explosions heard even at Jonesboro told Sherman that something was afoot in Atlanta. Either *Hood*, in preparation for leaving Atlanta, was attempting to destroy anything that might be useful to the Federals, or the Confederates had discovered and were attacking General Slocum's lone 20th Corps guarding the Chattahoochee River crossings. In fact, the Confederates were systematically blowing up a large amount of railroad rolling stock, including many boxcars of ammunition and great quantities of quartermaster and ordnance stores. By dawn of September 2, the work of destruction was done, and *Hood* had withdrawn his three corps down the McDonough Road to Lovejoy's Station, where they entrenched. After he determined the strength of this position by probing it with lines-of-battle, Sherman decided not to storm it directly.

During the previous night, the same explosions that had caught Sherman's ear near Jonesboro were also heard by General Slocum, who had been sending out details from his corps to test the strength of those Confederates still occupying Atlanta's defensive works. Early on the morning of the second, a reconnaissance force from the 20th Corps composed of several hundred infantry and dismounted cavalry under the command of Captain Henry M. Scott of the 70th Indiana Infantry was as usual advancing cautiously from the northwest toward the fortifications of Atlanta. Scott encountered James M. Calhoun, Atlanta's mayor, and a group of citizens who were carrying a flag of truce. Mayor Calhoun identified himself to Captain Scott and tendered the surrender of Atlanta. Calhoun was passed up the chain of command, and later that day officially surrendered the city in a note to General William T. Ward of the 20th Corps: "Sir: The fortune of war has placed Atlanta in your hands. As mayor of the city I ask protection to non-combatants and private property."

With Atlanta in his hands, a beaten enemy in his front, and his own men in need of a long rest, Sherman decided to end the campaign. He did so officially on September 8 after having wired Pres. Abraham Lincoln five days earlier: "Atlanta is ours, and fairly won." Sherman's Federals occupied the city through mid-November. Before departing, they destroyed whatever might have been useful to the Confederate government in continuing to use Atlanta in the war effort, and then they set out for Savannah on the infamous March to the Sea.

The Driving Tour of the Jonesboro Battlefield
(approximately 22.5 miles)

Go south from downtown on I-75. (Map 18) Where I-75/85 splits, be sure to continue on I-75 South. Take Exit 76, which is marked Jonesboro, and turn right onto Georgia Highway 54 (Jonesboro Road). Be sure to stay in the straight-only lanes at the traffic lights. Drive **3.5** miles south to Jonesboro. Highway 54 runs alongside the M&W roadbed. This railroad was the last of *Hood's* supply lines and was the object of Sherman's armies in late August. Just north of downtown Jonesboro, Highway 54 will turn right, but you should continue straight on Main Street alongside the railroad tracks. As you notice the stone depot coming up ahead on your left, look to the right and observe the Johnson-Blalock house. This house, built in the late 1840s, served as a makeshift hospital during the fighting around Jonesboro. Two blocks south of the depot (erected in 1868 to replace the one destroyed in 1864) turn right on College Street and go **.4** miles to where College ends at Fayetteville Road (Highway 54).

Around this intersection is the area where *Cleburne's* corps deployed for battle on August 31. They faced northwest toward the Federals of Howard's army on high ground a little over a half mile away. (The fateful gully was just in front of Howard's troops.) Turn right onto Fayetteville Road, drive **.8** miles to North Avenue (Highway 138), and turn left. For the past half mile, the road you have just traveled parallels the line of *Lee's* corps as it deployed for battle on the first day at Jonesboro. Staying on 138, cross over U.S. Highway 19/41 (Tara Boulevard). You are driving westward in the direction that *Lee's* corps attacked Howard's Army of the Tennessee.

Take the first left past U.S. 19/41. This will be Hynds Springs Road, which is just a short distance past a convenience store. As you drive through this neighborhood, you will be on a ridge that was occupied by portions of Logan's 15th Corps and Ransom's 16th Corps. The Federals here were attacked by elements of *Lee's* and *Cleburne's* Confederate corps, and the Union defenders held their ground primarily because of its advantageous elevation and the barricades that had been erected. The first road after you turn onto Hynds Springs is Dixon Road. Take a right onto Dixon, and continue till it ends at Magnolia Drive. Turn left there and stay on Magnolia, which curves to the left, for **.5** miles till you come to Holly Drive. As you drive along this road, you will notice that you are on high ground, ideally suited to protect troops from an

Looking northwest across U.S. Highway 41 toward the deep gully. The streambed which figured prominently in breaking up the Confederate divisions commanded by Gen. *Patrick R. Cleburne* during the first day's fighting is located at the base of the trees in the foreground. A portion of the ridge defended by the 15th and 16th Corps of General Howard's Army of the Tennessee is located in the background beyond the nearest trees. It is crowned by a line of trees on the horizon and marked by an arrow.

attack; that is precisely why this position was chosen by the Federals. The first part of Magnolia is only a few hundred yards east of the Flint River; then after the curve the deep gully that broke up the attack of *Cleburne's* Confederate corps will be on your right beyond the houses.

Turn left onto Holly Drive, travel its length, and turn right back onto Dixon Road. You are now facing eastward, the direction from which *Lee's* Confederates attacked. Turn left back onto Hynds Springs and then right onto Highway 138. (If you wish to view the Flint River and the area where a portion of Howard's army crossed, turn left on 138 and go .5 miles. After you cross the river turn around and go back east on 138.)

This next stage is a bit tricky, so be prepared. About .8 miles from Hynds Springs Road, Highway 138 will come to a "T" intersection with the railroad tracks directly in front of you. Turn left onto Highway 54 (Jonesboro Road), and then turn immediately right across the railroad tracks. As soon as you cross the tracks, the Confederate Cemetery will be on your left. There is an interesting historical marker just outside the cemetery gate. *Cleburne's* Confederate corps was positioned north of this immediate area when Davis's 14th Corps attacked south along the railroad tracks on the second day of the Battle of Jonesboro. Look

Looking northwest from the Confederate Cemetery on the north end of Jonesboro. In the distance through the trees the Warren House, a period structure which survived the Civil War and which figured prominently in the second day's battle, is visible. Beyond the house, Gen. *Daniel C. Govan's* brigade of General *Hardee's* Confederate corps was overrun on the second day of battle and substantially captured by elements of Union Gen. Jefferson C. Davis's 14th Corps.

A closer view of the Warren House, being renovated when this tour was published in the fall of 1984. (Photograph by J. Britt McCarley.)

to the northwest across the railroad and Highway 54 and observe the white, two-story Warren House, which was occupied by both sides at varying times and was in the thick of the second day's battle. Standing by the flagpole offers the best vantage point for the house. Near the Warren House, elements of the 14th Corps broke through the Southern line and captured Confederate General *Govan*, most of his brigade, and two artillery batteries. To the northeast, Stanley's 4th Corps approached the extreme right of *Hardee's* entrenched position at sundown on September 1. Sherman, greatly disappointed that Stanley's corps did not attack before darkness descended, believed that an excellent opportunity to surround and capture all of *Hardee's* troops had thus been lost. To leave the cemetery go back across the railroad as you came and turn right (north) on Highway 54. You may wish to observe the Warren House and the historical marker on your left soon after you get on Highway 54, which will return you to I-75. At I-75 cross the interstate bridge, follow the I-75 North signs, turn left onto the entrance ramp, and once on the expressway watch for the signs pointing north toward Atlanta. Your main tour is now complete.

Optional Tour of Jonesboro-Lovejoy Plantations
(approximately 17 miles)

In addition to the Warren House, there are quite a few other antebellum houses in and around Jonesboro.* While you are in the area you may wish to take this side tour that will take you by some of these residences and to several antebellum plantation homes that were in the vicinity of the Battle of Jonesboro and the cavalry action around Lovejoy.

Proceed south on McDonough Street from the cemetery to the intersection with Stockbridge Road (Highway 138). The house on the southeast corner was the wartime residence of Stephen Carnes, although the ornate porches and other changes are postwar additions. Carnes operated a wagon factory behind the house. During the war he produced caskets for the Confederate Army. Look across the railroad tracks and slightly to the north to observe the Johnson-Blalock House. This large residence, partially obscured by large magnolia trees, was built in the late 1840s. The house had columns at the time of the war, but the present ones may have been added shortly thereafter to repair wartime damage. During the war the Johnson family allowed Confederate supplies to be stored in the house, and wounded soldiers from the Battle of Jonesboro were treated there.

A block south of the Carnes House, at the corner of McDonough and King Streets, is the two-story brick Clayton County courthouse that was built in 1869 on the site of the one destroyed by Gen. Judson Kilpatrick's cavalry raiders in 1864. Behind the former courthouse, now used as a Masonic Lodge, is the old county jail built the same year.

Ahead and across the tracks stands the stone 1867 depot. It was constructed to replace a wooden one, which stood near the Confederate cemetery and was burned by Kilpatrick.

Continue south on McDonough Street. About three blocks south of the present courthouse (on your left just past the depot), McDonough Street curves and becomes Jodeco Road. Just after you round the curve, turn left into the parking lot of the Jonesboro Recreation Center

---

* This addendum was prepared by Bradley R. Rice drawing mainly from Alice C. Kilgore et al., eds., *History of Clayton County, Georgia, 1821-1983* (College Park: Ancestors Unlimited, Inc., 1983). The historic overview by Joseph Moore is especially helpful.

The Crawford-Talmadge House.

The Fitzgerald House.

to view the Stately Oaks plantation house (east and slightly behind the recreation building).

Built in 1839-40 in the Greek Revival style, Stately Oaks originally sat about four miles north of Jonesboro near the battle action. After it was moved to its present location in 1972, it was restored by Historic Jonesboro, Inc.*

Return as you came on Jodeco Road and McDonough Street for about .3 miles to College Street. Turn left across the tracks and then turn immediately left again onto Main Street (Highway 3). Go south 3 miles to the intersection with U.S Highway 19/41. Turn left on 19/41 and go **3.5** miles to Talmadge Road. (Note the stone marker that says Talmadge Farms.) Go **.5** miles down this lane (bearing left at the fork) to observe the Crawford-Talmadge and Fitzgerald homes which are in Henry County.

The Crawford-Talmadge place (on the left), built in 1835, was considerably enlarged and enhanced with the columned porch in the late 1850s. Thomas Crawford owned forty-six slaves and well over a thousand acres in 1860. The grand home was situated on the fringes of the military action in the Lovejoy area.

Across the road is the Fitzgerald House. It was originally located several miles north but was moved to this location in 1981. The plain style of this structure is typical of Piedmont plantation homes. Margaret Mitchell's great grandfather, Philip Fitzgerald, acquired the property in the 1830s, and Mitchell is said to have gathered some of the inspiration for *Gone With the Wind* from her many visits here, although neither this nor any of the other extant Clayton-Henry County plantation homes should be regarded as the fictional "Tara." Despite the plain appearance of the house, Fitzgerald was a well-to-do planter with thirty-five slaves and over 2,500 acres along the Flint River in 1860. (Both houses are currently owned by Betty Shingler Talmadge.)

---

* Two additional antebellum homes can be viewed farther out Jodeco Road. The Camp plantation, .9 miles east of Stately Oaks, was a refuge for many Jonesboro residents during the battle. The exterior appears much as it did in 1860. Go 1 mile to Carnes Road, turn right, and go .6 miles to see the Allen-Carnes place, the main part of which dates from the 1820s. There was an original porch, but Stephen Carnes added the present ornate one shortly after the war. Return to Stately Oaks to continue the main tour.

Forces Engaged
in the
Battles around Atlanta

The Battle of Peachtree Creek
July 20, 1864

FORCES ENGAGED (Only those forces specifically mentioned in the Peachtree Creek text have been included in this list.)

Confederates—General John B. Hood
Lieutenant-General Alexander P. Stewart's Corps
  Major-General Samuel G. French's Division—in reserve on the far left.
  Major-General Edward C. Walthall's Division
  Major-General William W. Loring's Division
Lieutenant-General William J. Hardee's Corps
  Brigadier-General George Maney's Division
  Major-General William H. T. Walker's Division
  Major-General William B. Bate's Division
  Major-General Patrick R. Cleburne's Division—in reserve in the center.
Major-General Benjamin F. Cheatham's Corps—fighting east of Atlanta and opposing McPherson's and Schofield's Federals.
Major-General Joseph Wheeler's Cavalry Corps—fighting with Cheatham's Confederates east of Atlanta.

Federals—Major-General William T. Sherman
Major-General George H. Thomas's Army of the Cumberland
  Major-General John M. Palmer's 14th Army Corps—only lightly engaged.
  Major-General Joseph Hooker's 20th Army Corps
    Brigadier-General Alpheus S. Williams's Division
    Brigadier-General John W. Geary's Division
      33d New Jersey Infantry Regiment
    Brigadier-General William T. Ward's Division—arrived during the battle.
  Major-General Oliver O. Howard's 4th Army Corps
    Brigadier-General John Newton's Division—detached from the corps and under direct command of Thomas.
Major-General John M. Schofield's Army of the Ohio—fighting northeast of Atlanta.
Major-General James B. McPherson's Army of the Tennessee—fighting east of Atlanta.

The Battle of Atlanta
July 22, 1864

FORCES ENGAGED (Only those forces specifically mentioned in the Atlanta text have been included in this list.)

Confederates—General John B. Hood
Lieutenant-General William J. Hardee's Corps
  Brigadier-General George Maney's Division
  Major-General Patrick R. Cleburne's Division
    Brigadier-General James A. Smith's Brigade
  Major-General William H. T. Walker's Division—upon Walker's death, division under command of Brigadier-General Hugh W. Mercer.
  Major-General William B. Bate's Division
Major-General Benjamin F. Cheatham's Corps
  Major-General Carter L. Stevenson's Division
  Brigadier-General John C. Brown's Division
    Brigadier-General Arthur M. Manigault's Brigade
    10th and 19th South Carolina Infantry Regiments and 28th Alabama Infantry Regiment
  Major-General Henry D. Clayton's Division
Lieutenant-General Alexander P. Stewart's Corps—not engaged.
Major-General Joseph Wheeler's Cavalry Corps—fighting at Decatur.

Federals—Major-General William T. Sherman
Major-General James B. McPherson's Army of the Tennessee—McPherson was killed during the battle, and the 15th Corps commander, John A. Logan, took over till July 27.
  Major-General John A. Logan's 15th Army Corps—M. L. Smith assumed temporary command when Logan replaced the deceased McPherson.
    Brigadier-General Charles R. Woods's Division
      Colonel Hugo Wangelin's Brigade
    Brigadier-General Morgan L. Smith's Division
      Colonel James S. Martin's Brigade
    Brigadier-General Joseph A. J. Lightburn's Brigade
      Battery H, 1st Illinois Light Artillery—Captain Francis De Gress.
      Battery A, 1st Illinois Light Artillery
    Brigadier-General William Harrow's Division
      Brigadier-General Charles C. Walcutt's Brigade
  Major-General Grenville M. Dodge's 16th Army Corps
    Brigadier-General Thomas W. Sweeny's Division
      Brigadier-General Elliott W. Rice's Brigade
      Colonel August Mersy's Brigade
    Brigadier-General John W. Fuller's Division
      Colonel John Morrill's Brigade
      Brigadier-General John W. Sprague's Brigade—fighting at Decatur.
      Ohio Light Artillery, 14th Battery
  Major-General Frank P. Blair, Jr.'s, 17th Army Corps

Brigadier-General Mortimer D. Leggett's Division
Brigadier-General Giles A. Smith's Division
Major-General George H. Thomas's Army of the Cumberland—not engaged.
Major-General John M. Schofield's Army of the Ohio—only lightly engaged.
Brigadier-General Kenner Garrard's Division—raiding Covington.

The Battle of Ezra Church
July 28, 1864

FORCES ENGAGED (Only those forces specifically mentioned in the Ezra Church text have been included in this list.)

Confederates—General John B. Hood
Lieutenant-General Stephen D. Lee's Corps
  Major-General Henry D. Clayton's Division
    Brigadier-General Randall L. Gibson's Brigade
    Brigadier-General Alpheus Baker's Brigade
  Brigadier-General John C. Brown's Division
Lieutenant-General Alexander P. Stewart's Corps—Walthall took over when Stewart was wounded.
  Major-General Edward C. Walthall's Division—Brigadier-General William A. Quarles took over the division when Walthall took temporary command of the corps.
  Major-General William W. Loring's Division—deployed but not engaged.

Federals—Major-General William T. Sherman
Major-General Oliver O. Howard's Army of the Tennessee
  Major-General John A. Logan's 15th Army Corps
    Brigadier-General Charles R. Woods's Division
      Colonel Hugo Wangelin's Brigade
    Brigadier-General Morgan L. Smith's Division
    Brigadier-General William Harrow's Division
      Colonel John M. Oliver's Brigade
      Brigadier-General Charles C. Walcutt's Brigade
        103rd Illinois Infantry Regiment, 97th Indiana Infantry Regiment, and 46th Ohio Infantry Regiment
  Major-General Grenville M. Dodge's 16th Army Corps—not engaged.
  Major-General Frank P. Blair, Jr.'s, 17th Army Corps—not engaged.
Major-General George H. Thomas's Army of the Cumberland
  Major-General John M. Palmer's 14th Army Corps
    Brigadier-General Jefferson C. Davis's Division—temporarily under the command of Brigadier-General James D. Morgan.
Major-General John M. Schofield's Army of the Ohio—only lightly engaged.

The Battle of Jonesboro
August 31–September 1, 1864

FORCES ENGAGED (Only those forces specifically mentioned in the Jonesboro text have been included in this list.)

Confederates—General John B. Hood
Lieutenant-General Stephen D. Lee's Corps
  Major-General Patton Anderson's Division
  Major-General Carter L. Stevenson's Division
  Major-General Henry D. Clayton's Division
Lieutenant-General William J. Hardee's Corps—Hardee was in overall command of his corps and Lee's, while Cleburne temporarily directed Hardee's corps.
  Brigadier-General Mark P. Lowrey's Division
  Brigadier-General John C. Brown's Division
  Major-General Patrick R. Cleburne's Division—under the command of Brigadier-General George Maney at Jonesboro, while Cleburne temporarily commanded Hardee's Corps.
    Brigadier-General Daniel C. Govan's Brigade
Major-General Joseph Wheeler's Cavalry Corps
  Brigadier-General William H. Jackson's Division

Federals—Major-General William T. Sherman
Major-General Oliver O. Howard's Army of the Tennessee
  Major-General John A. Logan's 15th Army Corps
  Brigadier-General Thomas E. G. Ransom's 16th Army Corps
  Major-General Frank P. Blair, Jr.'s, 17th Army Corps
Major-General George H. Thomas's Army of the Cumberland
  Major-General David S. Stanley's 4th Army Corps
  Brevet Major-General Jefferson C. Davis's 14th Army Corps
  Major-General Henry W. Slocum's 20th Army Corps
    Brigadier-General William T. Ward's Division
      Colonel John Coburn's Brigade
        70th Indiana Infantry Regiment
          Captain Henry M. Scott
  Major-General John M. Schofield's Army of the Ohio
Brigadier-General Judson Kilpatrick's Division

A Reader's Guide to the Atlanta Campaign

By Stephen Davis and Richard M. McMurry

The four major battles around Atlanta brought an end to the long campaign that had begun months before in the mountains just outside Chattanooga. When Gen. William T. Sherman set his Federal armies marching in early May 1864, he initiated a set of complicated military operations that still invite serious study. Civil War enthusiasts of all kinds—buffs, avocational historians, and professional scholars—continue to debate the major questions of the campaign: Did the Confederates ever have a real chance of stopping Sherman's armies? Could Confederate Gen. Joseph E. Johnston have been more aggressive in north Georgia? Did President Davis blunder in appointing John B. Hood to command the Southern army? Could the Confederates have held Atlanta once Sherman crossed the Chattahoochee?

These perplexing questions have challenged writers ranging from the very generals who commanded the opposing armies to more recent historians. Today there is a vast and varied literature on the campaign. This body of work includes the memoirs and biographies of the army commanders as well as numerous diaries, reminiscences, and collections of letters from both officers and enlisted men. Regimental histories by both participants and later writers provide close-up views of the campaign. The periodical literature is also plentiful, especially in such publications as *Civil War History, Civil War Times Illustrated,* the *Georgia Historical Quarterly,* and the *Atlanta Historical Journal* (formerly the *Atlanta Historical Bulletin*). Hereafter, these journals will be referred to as *CWH, CWTI, GHQ, AHJ,* and *AHB.*

While general histories of the Civil War usually cover the fight for Atlanta in a chapter or so, few volumes have been devoted exclusively to the history of the campaign. One of Sherman's officers, Gen. Jacob D. Cox, wrote the first full treatment of the subject for Scribner's *Campaigns of the Civil War* series. Cox's *Atlanta* (New York, 1882) is still readable and useful, though dated. Its focus on the Federal army, and especially on his own command, sometimes results in a neglect of other important aspects of the campaign.

Cox's work remained the only book-length study of the entire campaign until the publication of Samuel Carter III's *The Siege of Atlanta, 1864* (New York, 1973). Carter uses a variety of sources to tell his story "whenever possible from the standpoint of eyewitnesses or those who were close to the events." The result is a quick-paced and appealing narrative with lively commentaries, especially by Atlantans who endured the siege. When dealing with the campaign, however, Carter avoids analysis, and his work is sometimes undependable. In describing the Battle of Peachtree Creek, for instance, he relies too heavily on General Hood's reports, even implying, as Hood had charged, that Gen. William J. Hardee's Confederate corps failed to attack the enemy. There are also outright mistakes, such as Carter's statement that Confederate Gen. W. H. T. Walker was killed by Southern, rather than Union, pickets during the Battle of Atlanta.

Earl Schenck Miers's *The General Who Marched to Hell* (New York, 1951) is an interesting, broad treatment of the Atlanta Campaign, Sherman's March to the Sea, and the Union campaign as far as Columbia, South Carolina. Like Carter, Miers quotes generously from contemporary accounts. Readers might mistake the book for a biography of Sherman because of its title—in which "Hell" refers to the burning of Columbia in February 1865.

Detailed, critical, and more-or-less balanced accounts of the campaign may be found in two unpublished doctoral dissertations. That of Richard Manning McMurry, "The Atlanta Campaign, December 23, 1863, to July 18, 1864" (Emory University, 1967), takes the story up to Hood's accession to command. The narrative is continued by Errol MacGregor Clauss in "The Atlanta Campaign, 18 July-2 September 1864" (Emory University, 1965). (Copies of both dissertations are also available at the Atlanta Historical Society and through University Microfilms, Ann Arbor, Michigan.) McMurry's work led subsequently to the publication of *The Road Past Kennesaw: The Atlanta Campaign of 1864*, which was issued by the National Park Service in 1972. This booklet, with good maps and a photographic section, is useful as an introduction to the campaign. Much less successful is William Key's *The Battle of Atlanta and the Georgia Campaign* (New York, 1958)—a short account that is dramatic, but lacking in depth and insight.

One of the first scholarly overviews and still reliable is Thomas Robson Hay's "The Atlanta Campaign," *GHQ* 7(1923):19-43ff. A special issue of *CWTI* (July 1964) is devoted to the campaign for Atlanta; it includes articles by Allen P. Julian, Wilbur G. Kurtz, Bell I. Wiley, and Franklin M. Garrett, plus numerous pictures. Alan Keller's "On the Road to Atlanta: Johnston vs. Sherman," in *CWTI* (December 1962) offers a nicely readable summary of events up to Hood's assumption of command. George C. Osborn, in "The Atlanta Campaign, 1864," *GHQ* 34(1950):271-87, is too general. The histories of the various counties through which the armies passed and Franklin Garrett's *Atlanta and*

Environs also have sections about the war in Georgia.

The definitive study of the struggle for Atlanta has yet to be published, but Albert Castel is at work on a book that may eventually meet this need. Castel, professor of history at Western Michigan University, has published widely on the Civil War in the West.

The life of civilians during the campaign has received less attention than has been given to military events, but one very good book deals with the subject. In *Last Train From Atlanta* (New York, 1958), A.A. Hoehling gives us an interesting look at how the people of Atlanta lived as Sherman's armies closed in on the city. For the period of July 3 to September 15, 1864, Hoehling provides a "recital of little things that transpire in a city under siege," using contemporary observations and anecdotes gleaned from newspapers, letters, and memoirs. Hoehling manages to mold this quoted material into an absorbing account. The experiences of the state's citizenry in 1864 are also related as part of T. Conn Bryan's *Confederate Georgia* (Athens, 1953). The article by Philip Secrist, "Life in Atlanta," *CWTI* (July 1970), is accompanied by drawings and paintings by well-known Atlanta artist and historian Wilbur Kurtz. Appearing in a special issue of the *Atlanta Historical Journal* on "Atlanta in the Civil War" (Vol. 23, Summer 1979), is Robert Gibbon's "Life at the Crossroads of the Confederacy: Atlanta, 1861-1865." An unpublished doctoral dissertation by Ralph Benjamin Singer, Jr., "Confederate Atlanta" (University of Georgia, 1973), is also available at the Atlanta Historical Society and from University Microfilms.

For broad perspective on the army that defended Atlanta, one should consult Stanley F. Horn's *The Army of Tennessee* (Indianapolis, 1941; Norman, Okla., 1953). An energetic and solid study, Horn's book devotes fifty pages to the Atlanta Campaign and provides a good introduction to the controversies surrounding Confederate strategy. Horn defends Johnston's policy of avoiding a major battle in north Georgia while trading territory for time and tactical advantage. Although he justifies President Davis's removal of Johnston from command, Horn wonders if, by the time the change was made on July 17, 1864, the Confederates could have done anything to save Atlanta.

Thomas Lawrence Connelly's *Autumn of Glory: The Army of Tennessee, 1862-1865* (Baton Rouge, 1971) provides extensive and sophisticated coverage of the Southern army and is the most thoughtful assessment of the Confederate side of the Atlanta Campaign. Connelly places great emphasis on the rivalries, ambitions, and pettiness of high-ranking Southerners and the extent to which such factors constantly hampered the performance of their army. Connelly's opinions of the generals are frequently harsh, but his judgments on larger issues are often balanced and fair. For example, he concludes that Davis's removal of Johnston was "a costly error . . . though it seemed quite justified on the basis of evidence given to him." Especially perceptive is Connelly's examination of the wide-ranging consequences of the fall of Atlanta.

Larry Daniel's *Cannoneers in Gray* (Tuscaloosa, Alabama, forthcoming in 1984) will be a much-needed look at the important "long arm" of the Army of Tennessee's artillery throughout the war. A considerable portion of the work deals with the Atlanta Campaign.

A short, but useful, survey of many of the issues raised about the Confederate side of the campaign is made by Richard M. McMurry in "The Atlanta Campaign of 1864: A New Look," *CWH* 22(March 1976):5-15. Controversies among the southern leaders—especially the debate over the removal of Joseph E. Johnston—are explored in a number of articles, including those of Thomas Robson Hay, "Davis, Bragg, and Johnston in the Atlanta Campaign," *GHQ* 8(1924):38-48; Philip L. Secrist, "Prelude to the Atlanta Campaign: The Davis-Bragg-Johnston Controversy," *AHB* 17(Spring-Summer 1972); and Secrist, "Jefferson Davis and the Atlanta Campaign: A Study in Confederate Command," *AHB* 17(Fall-Winter 1972). McMurry, in "Confederate Morale in the Atlanta Campaign," *GHQ* 54(1970):226-43, argues that the "Johnston school" of historians has been misled and that Southern soldiers were, in fact, demoralized by "Old Joe's" constant retreats from Dalton to Atlanta. William J. McNeill's "A Survey of Confederate Soldier Morale During Sherman's Campaign Through Georgia and the Carolinas," *GHQ* 55(1971):1-25, represents the contrary view, maintaining that morale remained high under Johnston. Robert D. Little, in "General Hardee and the Atlanta Campaign," *GHQ* 29(1945):1-22, describes Hardee's role and defends him against Hood's allegations.

On the Federal side, the largest of Sherman's three armies is treated in Thomas B. Van Horne's *The History of the Army of the Cumberland* (two volumes and atlas, Cincinnati, 1875). There is no history of either the Army of the Tennessee or the Army of the Ohio.

Serious study of any Civil War military operation must come sooner or later to the *"O.R."*—the United States War Department's great compilation of *War of the Rebellion: Official Records of the Union and Confederate Armies* (Washington, 1880-1901). In over 100 bulky volumes, the government printed thousands of documents from both armies, such as after-action reports, letters, telegrams, orders, circulars, organizational tables, tabular strength reports, and casualty statements. The papers relating to the Atlanta Campaign are found in Series 1, Volume XXXVIII, parts 1-5, and in Volume LII, part 2. Excellent maps for the campaign and battles, with troop positions noted, are in the *O. R.* atlas (Washington, 1895).

Some very helpful topographical maps, keyed to modern streets, are printed in William R. Scaife, *Atlas of Atlanta Area Civil War Battles* (Atlanta, 1982). Also the *AHB* of September 1934 describes in fascinating detail the various Civil War sites around the city as they appeared in the 1930s. This work, with text by Franklin Garrett and Wilbur

Kurtz, keyed to I. U. Kauffman's map of the city, is still quite useful. Wartime letters and diaries provide much human interest material to supplement the *O. R.* and are indispensable in conveying the soldiers' thoughts and feelings. There are innumerable published accounts of this type and many more in manuscript repositories, including the Atlanta Historical Society and the Georgia Department of Archives and History. A few of the published works especially useful for the Atlanta Campaign are mentioned here. Several compilations pertain to Federals in the Atlanta Campaign: M. A. DeWolfe Howe, ed., *Home Letters of General Sherman* (New York, 1909); Rachael Sherman Thorndyke, ed., *The Sherman Letters: Correspondence Between General and Senator Sherman from 1837-1891* (New York, 1894); Milo M. Quaife, ed., *From the Cannon's Mouth: The Civil War Letters of General Alpheus S. Williams* (Detroit, 1959); K. Jack Bauer, ed., *Soldiering: The Civil War Diary of Rice C. Bull, 123rd New York Volunteer Infantry* (San Rafael, Calif., 1978); Paul M. Angle, ed., *Three Years in the Army of the Cumberland: The Letters and Diary of Major James A. Connolly* (Bloomington, 1959); and G. S. Bradley, ed., *The Star Corps: or Notes of an Army Chaplain During Sherman's Famous "March to the Sea"* (Milwaukee, 1865). A unique combination of two enemies' diaries is edited by Wirt Armistead Cate, *Two Soldiers: The Campaign Diaries of Thomas J. Key, C.S.A., December 7, 1863-May 17, 1865, and Robert J. Campbell, U.S.A., January 1, 1864-July 21, 1864* (Chapel Hill, 1938). Some Northerners' letters have appeared in the *GHQ*: Richard B. Harwell, ed., "The Campaign from Chattanooga to Atlanta as Seen by a Federal Soldier," 25(1941):262-78; James A. Padgett, ed., "With Sherman Through Georgia and the Carolinas: Letters of a Federal Soldier," 32(1948):284-322, and Arville L. Funk, ed., "A Hoosier Regiment in Georgia, 1864," 48(1964):104-9.

Notable letters and diaries on the Confederate side include W. M. Cash and L. S. Howorth, eds., *My Dear Nellie: The Civil War Letters of William L. Nugent to Eleanor Smith Nugent* (Jackson, Miss., 1977); and Mills Lane, ed., *"Dear Mother: Don't grieve about me. If I Get Killed, I'll only be Dead." Letters from Georgia Soldiers in the Civil War* (Savannah, 1977). Two dozen missives in Lane's collection pertain to the Atlanta Campaign. Especially colorful are "The Confederate Letters of John W. Hagan," edited by Bell Irvin Wiley, *GHQ* 38(1954):268-94. Sergeant Hagan's correspondence was reprinted as a booklet: Wiley, ed., *Confederate Letters of John W. Hagan* (Athens, 1954). Other letters of Southern soldiers are also to be found in the *GHQ*: George C. Osborn, ed., "Civil War Letters of Robert W. Banks: Atlanta Campaign" 27(1943):208-16; Donald W. Lewis, ed., "A Confederate Officer's Letters on Sherman's March to Atlanta" 51(1967):491-94; Elizabeth Hulsey Marshall, ed., "Watch on the Chattahoochee: A Civil War Letter" 43(1959):427-28; and Andrew Forest Muir, ed., "The Battle of Atlanta as Described by a Confederate Soldier" 42(1958):109-11. Delightful excerpts from the letters of a semi-literate Georgian named Angus McDermid are in Benjamin Rountree, ed., "Letters from a Confederate Soldier," *Georgia Review* 18(1964):267-97.

Civilians also recorded their experiences. Several letters from a soldier's wife who endured the siege of Atlanta are presented in Jane Bonner Peacock, ed., "A Wartime Story: The Davidson Letters, 1862-1865," *AHB* 19(Spring 1975). Also interesting is T. Conn Bryan's "A Georgia Woman's Civil War Diary: The Journal of Minerva Leah Rowles McClatchey, 1864-65," *GHQ* 51(1967):197-216. John Robert Smith has taken personal accounts from the archives of the Atlanta Historical Society and related citizens' impressions of "The Day Atlanta Was Occupied," *AHB* 21(Fall 1977). "Atlanta as Sherman Left It—Atlanta Then and Now," *AHB* 1(May 1930) is a reprint of an eyewitness report of the state of the city in mid-December 1864, with almost a house-by-house description of damage.

After the war many veterans wrote accounts of their service in the Atlanta Campaign. In examining these sources, readers should differentiate between letters or diaries written during the campaign and postwar reminiscences. Memoirs or autobiographies written years after the war are likely to be colored by hindsight and by "old soldierism"—the veterans' habit of romanticizing their military experiences. Generals who set down their recollections usually felt compelled to justify their war record, and frequently their narratives are self-aggrandizing.

Sherman, Johnston, and Hood all wrote books in which they dealt at greater or lesser length with the Atlanta Campaign. Sherman penned his *Memoirs* a decade after the war. The work was published in a two-volume edition and has been reprinted several times since, most notably by Indiana University Press in 1967. Mills Lane has excerpted that part of Sherman's *Memoirs* treating the struggle for Atlanta and the March to the Sea and reprinted it along with selections from the general's letters as *"War is Hell!": William T. Sherman's Personal Narrative of His March Through Georgia* (Savannah, 1974). The Federal commander's writing is usually straightforward and clear, and he seems to avoid much of the contentiousness and self-justification that mark the books of the Confederate leaders. As observers have noted, the victor in war can afford to be less bitter than his former enemies.

In his *Narrative of Military Operations* (New York, 1874; Bloomington, Ind., 1959), Gen. Joseph E. Johnston covers the Atlanta Campaign in seventy pages, giving almost as much attention to attacking his personal enemies, especially Hood and Davis, as he does to the military operations against the Yankees. John Bell Hood's *Advance and Retreat* (Philadelphia, 1880; Bloomington, 1959) includes a rebuttal against Johnston, whose policies, Hood asserted, led to the Confederate defeat despite all that Hood could do to offset them. A sympathetic view of

General Hood's memoir is given by David G. Chollett in "Advance and Retreat: Rage or Reason?" *AHB* 20(Spring 1976).

Some Federal generals besides Sherman also wrote reminiscences of their Civil War service, including material on Atlanta. John M. Schofield's *Forty-Six Years in the Army* (New York, 1897) and Jacob D. Cox's *Military Reminiscences of the Civil War* (New York, 1900) cover the Army of the Ohio. Oliver O. Howard's *Autobiography* (New York, 1907); William B. Hazen's *A Narrative of Military Service* (Boston, 1895); Richard W. Johnson's *A Soldier's Reminiscences in Peace and War* (Philadelphia, 1886); and David S. Stanley's *Personal Memoirs* (Cambridge, 1917) depict the campaign as it was remembered by four Union generals.

Besides Johnston and Hood, only two Confederate generals involved in the Atlanta Campaign left book-length accounts of their service. Samuel G. French's *Two Wars: An Autobiography* (Nashville, 1901) includes an account based on the diary French kept in 1864. *A Carolinian Goes to War: The Civil War Narrative of Arthur Middleton Manigault, Brigadier General, C.S.A.* (Columbia, S.C., 1983, edited by R. Lockwood Tower) gives excellent details on the operation of Manigault's brigade in 1864 as well as some valuable views of the Confederate side of the campaign.

There are two very useful collections of writings by participants in the campaign. Robert Underwood Johnson and Clarence Clough Buell edited a massive array of reminiscences in *Battles and Leaders of the Civil War* (4 vols., New York, 1887, 1956). Eight articles on the Atlanta Campaign, including ones written by Sherman, Johnston, and Hood, appear in volume four. A number of Federal officers' reminiscences of the campaign have been collected by Sydney C. Kerksis and printed as the *Atlanta Papers* (Dayton, Ohio, 1980). Most of the thirty papers were read in the 1880s and 1890s at veterans' gatherings. An important address not included in this collection is Mortimer D. Leggett's "The Battle of Atlanta" (1883), delivered before the Society of the Army of the Tennessee. General Leggett commanded a Union division in the thickest of the fighting on July 22.

Memoirs by lower-ranking officers and enlisted men are numerous. The quality of these writings varies widely. Some are little more than lists of the battles in which the writer participated; others are detailed chronicles based on wartime letters or diaries, sometimes supplemented with material from the *Official Records*. A sampling of the better Yankee narratives containing Atlanta material would include those of Charles W. Wills, *Army Life of an Illinois Soldier* (Washington, 1906); John A. Joyce, *A Checkered Life* (Chicago, 1883); George W. Bailey, *A Private Chapter of the War* (St. Louis, 1880); and Theodore F. Upson, *With Sherman to the Sea* (edited by O. O. Winther; Bloomington, 1958).

Confederate accounts are fewer and, as a rule, less complete than those by the Federals. A roster of the better southern writings includes *Four Years on the Firing Line* (edited by Bell I. Wiley; Jackson, Tenn., 1963) by James Cooper Nisbet, who commanded the 66th Georgia until his capture on July 22; R. M. Collins, *Chapters from the Unwritten History of the War Between the States* (St. Louis, 1893); Albert D. Kirwan, ed., *Johnny Green of the Orphan Brigade: The Journal of a Confederate Soldier* (Lexington, Ky., 1956); and Walter A. Clark, *Under the Stars and Bars: or Memories of Four Years Service with the Oglethorpes, of Augusta, Georgia* (Augusta, 1900). Less reliable but far better known is Sam Watkins's *Co. Aytch, Maury Grays, First Tennessee Regiment or a Side Show of the Big Show* (Chattanooga, 1900). The reminiscences of a well-educated Georgian are provided in Lilla Mills Hawes, ed., "The Memoirs of Charles H. Olmstead," in the *GHQ*. The tenth and eleventh installments, dealing with the Atlanta Campaign, appear in Volumes 44(1960):419-34, and 45(1961):42-56.

Two other works should be mentioned. Kate Cumming's *A Journal of Hospital Life in the Confederate Army of Tennessee from the Battle of Shiloh to the End of the War* (Louisville, 1866) has been reprinted as *Kate: The Journal of a Confederate Nurse*, edited by Richard B. Harwell (Baton Rouge, 1959). A civilian's experiences during the summer of 1864 are described in Mary A. H. Gay's *Life in Dixie During the War* (Atlanta, 1894, 1979). Miss Gay lived in Decatur.

As with personal narratives, regimental histories by Federals are more numerous than such works by Southerners. Among the worthwhile Union regimentals are Benjamin F. Magee's *History of the 72nd Indiana* (Lafayette, 1882); Samuel Merrill's *The Seventh Indiana Volunteer Infantry in the War of the Rebellion* (Indianapolis, 1900); William W. Belknap's *History of the Fifteenth Regiment Iowa Veteran Volunteer Infantry* (Keokuk, 1887); Alexis Cope's *The Fifteenth Ohio Volunteers and Its Campaigns* (Columbus, 1916); Charles T. Clark's *Opdycke Tigers, the 125th O.V.I.: A History of the Regiment and of the Campaign and Battles of the Army of the Cumberland* (Columbus, 1895). Good modern treatments of Federal units are found in Leslie Ander's *The Eighteenth Missouri* (Indianapolis, 1968); and two books by John W. Rowell: *Yankee Cavalrymen: Through the Civil War with the Ninth Pennsylvania Cavalry* (Knoxville, 1971) and *Yankee Artillerymen: Through the Civil War with Eli Lilly's Indiana Battery* (Knoxville, 1975).

There are some good Confederate unit histories: W. J. McMurray's *History of the Twentieth Tennessee Regiment Volunteer Infantry, C.S.A.* (Nashville, 1904); Ephraim McD. Anderson's *Memoirs Historical and Personal Including the Campaign of the First Missouri Confederate Brigade* (St. Louis, 1868; Dayton, Ohio, 1972); and William C. Davis's *The Orphan Brigade: The Kentucky Confederates Who Couldn't Go Home* (New York, 1980).

Charles E. Dornbusch's *Regimental Publications and Personal Narratives of the Civil War: A Checklist* (New York, 1961) is a helpful guide for many of the older accounts. Some other unit histories are listed in Allan Nevins, James I. Robertson, Jr., and Bell I. Wiley, eds., *Civil War Books: A Bibliography*, 2 vols. (Baton Rouge, 1967 and 1969).

Another good way to approach the campaign is through the biographies of the generals who participated in it. There have been many studies of William T. Sherman. By far the best place to start is Albert Castel's three-part article, "The Life of a Rising Son," published in *CWTI* in July, August, and October 1979. Providing a view of Sherman as battle captain is Basil Henry Liddell Hart's *Sherman: Soldier, Realist, American* (New York, 1929). Lloyd Lewis's *Sherman, Fighting Prophet* (New York, 1932) remains the best work on the Union general. James M. Merrill's *William Tecumseh Sherman* (New York, 1971) is a semi-psychological profile using materials unavailable to earlier biographers, but the book contains factual errors and is weak in analysis of military operations. John Bennett Walters, in *Merchant of Terror: General Sherman and Total War* (Indianapolis, 1973), emphasizes Sherman's devastation of southern resources in his campaigns. E. Merton Coulter's "Sherman and the South," *GHQ* 15(1931):28-45, is a more sympathetic view of the Yankee general by the late dean of Georgia historians.

One of the best short accounts of the campaign from the Federal perspective is found in Francis F. McKinney's *Education in Violence: The Life of George H. Thomas and the History of the Army of the Cumberland* (Detroit, 1961). Thomas was Sherman's chief subordinate during the campaign, and his command embraced two-thirds of the Union troops involved. Thomas is also covered by Freeman Cleaves in *Rock of Chickamauga: The Life of General George H. Thomas* (Norman, Okla., 1948) and by Wilbur Thomas in *General George H. Thomas, the Indomitable Warrior* (New York, 1964). Readers should be aware that much of the material written by and about the high-ranking Federals was part of a debate that raged for several decades between partisans of Thomas and Sherman. Principally the argument involved the extent to which Thomas deserved credit for the successes attributed to Sherman. For example, Henry Stone's "The Atlanta Campaign," in the Military Historical Society of Massachusetts *Papers* 8(1910):341-492, belongs to the pro-Thomas, anti-Sherman school.

Recent biographies of Yankee leaders prominent in the Atlanta Campaign are those of James L. McDonough, *Schofield: Union General in the Civil War and Reconstruction* (Tallahassee, 1972); John A. Carpenter, *Sword and Olive Branch: Oliver Otis Howard* (Pittsburgh, 1964); James P. Jones, *"Black Jack": John A. Logan and Southern Illinois in the Civil War* (Tallahassee, 1967); and Stanley P. Hirshson, *Grenville M. Dodge: Soldier, Politician, Railroad Pioneer* (Bloomington, 1967).

An introduction to Gen. James B. McPherson, who commanded the Union Army of the Tennessee until his death in the Battle of Atlanta, is provided by William W. Hassler's article, "A Sunny Temper and a Warm Heart," *CWTI* (November 1967). Elizabeth J. Whaley's *Forgotten Hero: General James B. McPherson* (New York, 1955) is inadequate in treating this important Federal officer. James P. Jones, in "General Jeff C. Davis, U.S.A., and Sherman's Georgia Campaign," *GHQ* 47(1963):231-48, reviews the service of one of Sherman's division leaders.

Joseph E. Johnston, the first of the two Confederate commanders in the campaign, lacks a good modern biography. Gilbert E. Govan and James W. Livingood in *A Different Valor: The Story of General Joseph E. Johnston, C.S.A.* (Indianapolis, 1956) tell of his life, but the book is flawed by the authors' uncritical acceptance of Johnston's position in his quarrels with Davis and Hood. Still valuable is Alfred P. James's article, "General Joseph E. Johnston, Storm Center of the Confederate Army," *Mississippi Valley Historical Review* 14(1927-28):342-59. More up to date is Richard M. McMurry's " 'The *Enemy* at Richmond': Joseph E. Johnston and the Confederate Government," *CWH* 27(1981):5-31.

Johnston's successor has been treated by John P. Dyer in *The Gallant Hood* (New York, 1950), a work which is superficial in its description of the Atlanta Campaign but which is better than Richard O'Connor's *Hood, Cavalier General* (New York, 1949). Richard M. McMurry's *John Bell Hood and the War for Southern Independence* (Lexington, Ky., 1982) is a recent study, with three of its twelve chapters devoted to the Atlanta Campaign.

The life of one of the best and most tragic of all Confederate military leaders is described in Irving A. Buck's *Cleburne and His Command* (1908; Jackson, Tenn., 1958) and in Howell and Elizabeth Purdues' *Pat Cleburne, Confederate General: A Definitive Biography* (Hillsboro, Tex., 1973). Buck was a member of Cleburne's staff, and his account is far better, although less detailed, than that of the Purdues. Other leading Confederates are covered by Nathaniel Cheairs Hughes, Jr., in *General William J. Hardee: Old Reliable* (Baton Rouge, 1965); Joseph H. Parks in *General Leonidas Polk, C.S.A.: The Fighting Bishop* (Baton Rouge, 1962); and John P. Dyer in *From Shiloh to San Juan: The Life of "Fightin' Joe" Wheeler* (Baton Rouge, 1941, rev. ed. 1961). Herman Hattaway's *General Stephen D. Lee* (Jackson, Miss., 1976) is an excellent study of the officer who assumed command of Hood's corps. Less effective is Marshall Wingfield's *General A. P. Stewart: His Life and Letters* (Memphis, 1954); Stewart took over Polk's corps in late June 1864.

Division commanders get shorter treatment, as in articles by Holman D. Jordan, "The Military Career of Henry D. Clayton," *Alabama Review* 13(1960):127-34, and Stephen Davis, "A Georgia Firebrand: Major

General W. H. T. Walker, C.S.A.," *GHQ* 63(1970):44-60. Karlem Riess, "Claudius Wistar Sears, Soldier and Educator," *Journal of Mississippi History* 11(1949):128-37, and Charles M. Cummings, "Otho French Strahl: 'Choicest Spirit to Embrace the South,' " *Tennessee Historical Quarterly* 24(1965):341-55, are short pieces on two brigadiers in the Army of Tennessee.

Brief sketches of every Federal and Confederate general have been studiously prepared by Ezra J. Warner in *Generals in Gray* (Baton Rouge, 1959) and *Generals in Blue* (Baton Rouge, 1964), two works especially valuable for their information on lesser-known officers.

Another category of writings addresses the particular battles and actions of the Atlanta Campaign. Richard M. McMurry's "The Opening Phase of the 1864 Campaign in the West," *AHJ* 27(Summer 1983), discusses the fighting in May around Dalton. In articles for *CWTI*, the same author has provided straightforward explanations of several more engagements: "Resaca: 'A Heap of Hard Fiten' " (November 1970); " 'The Hell Hole,' " on New Hope Church (February 1973); "The Affair at Kolb's Farm" (December 1968); and "Kennesaw Mountain" (January 1970). In "Cassville," *CWTI* (December 1971), McMurry evaluates the controversy surrounding Johnston's missed opportunity to strike a blow on May 19, 1864. Philip Secrist's "Resaca: For Sherman a Moment of Truth," *AHJ* 22(Spring 1978) is a detailed account of that battle. Morton R. McInvale's *The Battle of Pickett's Mill: "Foredoomed to Oblivion"* (Atlanta, 1977) is an interesting booklet relating the small battle of May 27, fought near New Hope Church. Philip L. Secrist has covered the same fight in "Scenes of Awful Carnage," *CWTI* (June 1971). An article by Sydney C. Kerksis, "Action at Gilgal Church, Georgia, June 15-16, 1864," *AHB* 15(Fall 1970), is reprinted as an appendix to the *Atlanta Papers* cited above. McMurry's "More on Raw Courage," *CWTI* (October 1975), relates the encounter at the Chattahoochee River, July 9, between Confederate pickets and Federals who attacked in the nude.

The battles closer to Atlanta have also received attention. Steven J. Adolphson, in "An Incident of Valor in the Battle of Peach Tree Creek, 1864," in the *GHQ* 57(1973):406-20, tells how Col. Douglas Hapeman of the 104th Illinois won the Congressional Medal of Honor for leading a counterattack that helped blunt the Confederate advance. Bruce Catton's "The Battle of Atlanta," *Georgia Review* 10(1956):256-64, was reprinted from *American Heritage*. Wilbur Kurtz's painstaking research on the Battle of Atlanta is reflected in his article "The Death of Major-General W. H. T. Walker, July 22, 1864," *CWH* 6(1960):174-79. Errol MacGregor Clauss's "The Battle of Jonesborough," appears in *CWTI* (November 1968).

On cavalry operations, a good summary is Philip L. Secrist's "The Role of Cavalry in the Atlanta Campaign, 1864," *GHQ* 56(1972):510-28.

J. P. Dyer, in "Some Aspects of Cavalry Operations in the Army of Tennessee," *Journal of Southern History* 8(1942):210-25 [hereafter *JSH*] examines the ineffective use of Confederate cavalry in the campaign. The major Federal cavalry raid around Atlanta in late July 1864 is thoroughly treated by Byron H. Mathews in *The McCook-Stoneman Raid* (Philadelphia, 1976). The same operation is described in John W. Rowell's article, "McCook's Raid," in the July 1974 issue of *CWTI*. Stephen Starr's forthcoming volume three of *The Union Cavalry in the Civil War* will cover the mounted combat in Georgia during 1864.

The importance of railroads in the campaign is stressed by Armin E. Mruck in "The Role of Railroads in the Atlanta Campaign," *CWH* 7(1961):264-71, and by Errol Clauss in "Sherman's Rail Support in the Atlanta Campaign," *GHQ* 50(1966):413-20. Robert C. Black III, in "The Railroads of Georgia in the Confederate War Effort," *JSH* 13(1947):11-34, gives only brief mention of the Atlanta Campaign but relates good background on rail systems in the state. James G. Bogle treats the railway that supported both armies in northern Georgia in "The Western & Atlantic Railroad—1864," *AHJ* 25(Summer 1981). An unpublished master's thesis by J. Britt McCarley, " 'He Was So Well Provided for that He Could Sweep the World for Gain': The Supply of Sherman's Armies during the Atlanta Campaign, 1864" (Georgia State University, 1982) challenges the popular interpretation that Sherman's Federals lived off the north Georgia countryside during the march to Atlanta. His research correctly points out that the overwhelming proportion of the Union forces' subsistence was provided by their own internally organized and administered supply bureaus.

Several good articles address other topics: Bruce S. Eastwood's "Confederate Medical Problems in the Atlanta Campaign," *GHQ* 47(1963):276-92; James O. Breeden's "A Medical History of the Later Stages of the Atlanta Campaign," *JSH* 35(1969):31-59; Hartwell T. Bynum's "Sherman's Expulsion of the Roswell Women in 1864," *GHQ* 54(1970):169-82; and Wilbur G. Kurtz's "A Federal Spy in Atlanta," *AHB* 10, December 1957. Errol MacGregor Clauss, in "Sherman's Failure at Atlanta," *GHQ* 53(1969):321-29, argues that the Federals blundered in allowing Hood's army to escape the city on the night of September 1, 1864.

Complementing this extensive literature is an interesting pictorial record of the Atlanta Campaign. George N. Barnard's *Photographic Views of Sherman's Campaign* (New York, 1977) is the best single source of photographs featuring terrain and fortifications. Barnard's four photos of General Sherman, posing at a fort outside Atlanta after the fall of the city, are displayed in "Sherman Strikes a Pose," *CWTI* (January 1970). Many good photographs are collected in Volume III of Francis Trevelyan Miller, ed., *The Photographic History of the Civil War* (New York, 1911), and in William C. Davis, ed., *The Image of*

War, the new multivolume photographic history being published by the National Historical Society.

In another category are the wartime drawings of artist-correspondents whose pictures were engraved for publication in the northern illustrated weeklies. Theodore Davis, artist for *Harper's Weekly,* accompanied Sherman's army, and his sketches appear in Fletcher Pratt's *Civil War in Pictures* (Garden City, N.Y., 1955) and in Alfred H. Guernsey and Henry M. Alden's *Harper's Pictorial History of the Civil War* (New York, 1866; recently reprinted by Fairfax Press, New York). A number of drawings of Atlanta, made thirty years after the war by Edwin J. Meeker, Walton Taber, and others for *Battles and Leaders,* are excellently reproduced in Stephen W. Sears, ed., *The American Heritage Century Collection of Civil War Art* (New York, 1974).

Wilbur Kurtz's modern drawings and paintings about the Atlanta Campaign are famous for their technical merit and historical accuracy. A number of them appear in the booklet *Atlanta and the Old South: Paintings and Drawings by Wilbur G. Kurtz* (Atlanta, 1969). Of course, the most famous painting from the campaign is the Cyclorama, the 100-year-old, 360-degree panorama of the battle. Kurtz's booklet, *The Atlanta Cyclorama: The Story of the Famed Battle of Atlanta* (Atlanta, 1954), includes a full-color reproduction of the mural with details of its prominent features. Alma Hill Jamison's "A History of the Cyclorama," *Atlanta Historical Bulletin* 2 (July 1937) is a brief treatment which includes an explanation of the painting.

Sherman's occupation of Atlanta on September 2 brought an end to the long campaign. Here we have tried briefly to survey the important publications dealing with the struggle. No doubt a few works have been overlooked. In such cases, we would like to think that our oversight confirms what today's "Civil Warriors" are constantly finding: that the study of the Atlanta Campaign continues to provide opportunities for discovery and challenge.

A Look At The Latest Literature, 1984-1989

By Stephen Davis

Since the publication of "A Reader's Guide" in 1984, a number of noteworthy books or articles pertaining to the Atlanta Campaign have appeared.

James Lee McDonough and James Pickett Jones's *War So Terrible: Sherman and Atlanta* (New York, 1987) rates as the first book-length study of the campaign by professional historians. The authors' perspective on events is generally sound, and their argument for the superiority of Sherman's generalship over Johnston and Hood is persuasive. But students have discerned occasional errors in the text. More serious have been other scholars' allegations of plagiarism, which at the time of this writing have forced the publisher to withdraw the book from sales.

Soldiers' letters and diaries continue to be printed. Interesting diary entries by a confederate soldier in the 63d Georgia appear as "The Federal March through Georgia: An Account of Pvt. William Norrell," in the newly established *Journal of Confederate History* 1(1988):49-82. The Northern perspective is given in Lewis N. Wynne and Barbara Ann Grim, "On the Road to Atlanta: Observations of a Yankee Soldier," *Atlanta History: A Journal of Georgia and the South,* hereafter cited as *AH,* formerly the *Atlanta Historical Journal* 31 (Winter 1987-88), and in Albert Castel, ed., "Scouting, Foraging, and Skirmishing: The Federal Occupation of Atlanta as Seen in the Letters of Maj. William C. Stevens, Ninth Michigan Calvary," *AHJ,* 23(Summer 1979); 73-90. See McMurry and Davis's original reader's guide for other abbreviations.

The Confederate Army of Tennessee and its leaders remain attractive for study. Richard M. McMurry assesses the problems and weaknesses of the army defending Atlanta in *Two Great Rebel Armies: An Essay in Confederate Military History* (Chapel Hill, 1989), in which his point of comparison is Robert E. Lee's Army of Northern Virginia. Larry J. Daniel, author of *Cannoneers in Gray* (cited in our 1984 essay), is about to complete a book-length manuscript entitled *Soldiering in the Army of Tennessee: A Portrait of Life in a Confederate Army.* Brief biographical profiles of Confederate generals fighting in Georgia are given in McMurry's "Patton Anderson,

110

Major General, C.S.A.," *Blue & Gray*(October-November, 1983) [hereafter cited as *B&G*], and Dennis Kelly's "Back in the Saddle: The War Record of William Bate," *CWTI* (December 1988). In addition, a biography of Confederate Maj. Gen. Benjamin F. Cheatham, by Christopher Losson, is scheduled for publication by the University of Tennessee Press.

On military operations, see Roy Morris, Jr., and Phil Noblitt, "The History of a Failure" (regarding McPherson's Snake Creek Gap maneuver west of Resaca), *CWTI* (September 1988); D. Reid Ross, "Battle of Kolb's Farm: Its Relevance to Sherman's March on Atlanta," *AH* 32(Spring 1988); and H. David Williams, " 'On the Fringes of Hell': Billy Yank and Johnny Reb at the Seige of Kennesaw Mountain," *GHQ* 70(1986):703-716. See also Albert Castel's article on the fighting west of Atlanta during August 4 through August 6, 1864, "Union Fizzle at Atlanta: The Battle of Utoy Creek," *CWTI* (February 1978).

Confederate Gen. Joseph Wheeler's cavalry strike at Decatur on July 22, is treated in David Evans's "The Fight for the Wagons," *CWTI*(February 1988). On other cavalry operations, see William Harris Bragg, "The General Lost in Georgia" (on the McCook-Stoneman Raid), *CWTI* (June 1985); and James Hibbard and Albert Castel, "Kilpatrick's Jonesboro Raid, August 18-22, 1864," *AHJ* 29(Summer 1985). A novel treatment of the Confederate cavalry raid into north Georgia and Tennessee, August 1864, is Lewis A. Lawson's *Wheeler's Last Raid* (Greenwood, Fla., 1986), in which the author's research is presented in the form of a fictitious Confederate soldier's diary.

During 1989, *Blue & Gray* magazine will release three special issues devoted to the Atlanta Campaign. Richard McMurry will review military events up to early June 1864 (for the April 1989 issue); to be included is Jeff Dean's study of the battle of Pickett's Mill. Kennesaw Mountain Park historian Dennis Kelly will cover operations from Pine Mountain to the Chattahoochee River (June issue), and Stephen Davis writes on the fighting around Atlanta and the city's fall in *B&G* for August '89. Each issue will contain up-to-date maps and recommended driving tours.

Other recent articles of interest are Marlin G. Kime, "Sherman's Gordian Knot: Logistical Problems in the Atlanta Campaign," *GHQ*70(1986):102-110; and David Evans, "Wool, Women and War" (on the explusion of the Roswell women), *CWTI* (September 1987). The fiftieth anniversary of the publication of Margaret Mitchell's *Gone With the Wind* in 1986 prompted reexamination of the famous novel by Civil War historians. Prof. James P. Jones assesses Miss Mitchell's work in the final chapter of *War So Terrible*, cited above. A good analysis of the novel's historical content is Albert Castel's " 'I didn't want to get caught out...,' or *Gone With the Wind* as History," *B&G*(July 1986). A more general treatment is found in Roy Meador's "50 Years of *Gone With the Wind*," *CWTI* (September 1986).

INDEX